CROSS-EXAMINING PSYCHIATRISTS AND PSYCHOLOGISTS

ALAN T. RADNOR

CROSS-EXAMINING PSYCHIATRISTS AND PSYCHOLOGISTS

A PRACTICAL GUIDE

Cover design by Monica Alejo/ABA Publishing.

Printed in the United States of America.

18 17 16 15 14 5 4 3 2 1

ISBN: 978-1-62722-856-5
e-ISBN: 978-1-62722-857-2

Library of Congress Cataloging-in-Publication Data is on file with the Library of Congress

To Carol

Contents

PREFACE

This is a book about cross-examining psychiatrists and psychologists in civil cases. Similar to my book *Cross-Examining Doctors: A Practical Guide*, Second Edition (ALI ABA, 2010), this is a book of experience. As in that book, I have used real transcripts, unedited, to demonstrate the good and not-so-good approaches to cross-examination.

I was trained in a traditional, large Midwestern law firm with a large trial practice. I had the benefit of senior trial lawyer mentors who had tried hundreds of jury trials. I was taking expert depositions during my first year at the firm and trying cases as first chair within two years. Sadly, those opportunities do not exist today. Few lawyers have 100 jury trials in civil practice, and it is well-documented that fewer opportunities to try cases exist today.[1]

My effort here is to preserve some of the knowledge, techniques, and approaches of lawyers with vast experience. Preserving this record of transcripts will enable those of us who have less experience because of the circumstances of today's practice to have the benefit of our predecessors' thinking on these issues. Actual transcripts, raw though they may be, show how it looks in actual practice without authorial shaping of questions and answers. Such reshaping reads well and is entertaining but does not reflect actual practice. One historical transcript has been included here: the cross-examination of Dr. Binger in the Alger Hiss Trial of 1950. It illustrates some of the approaches addressed in this book but also shows that these successful approaches have not changed over the decades.

As noted, these are civil cases. My firm had a large workers' compensation practice, so those transcripts are included, along with an equal

1. Ad Hoc Committee on the Future of the Civil Trial, American College of Trial Lawyers. *The "Vanishing Trial," the College, the Profession, the Civil Justice System*, Fed. Rules Decisions, 226, 414 (2004).

number of personal injury case transcripts involving psychological claims and issues. Most of these transcripts are from my firm but, to create some balance, I have also included transcripts of cross-examinations by other highly skilled lawyers. I have placed more emphasis on substantive areas of cross-examination than on technique, although technique is always a part of the skill set. The focus here on substantive areas is driven by the somewhat unique position that psychiatrists' and psychologists' opinions hold in the medical/legal world. First, their opinions, although sometimes based on testing, are primarily based on the subjective activity of talking to their patients. Therefore, the accuracy of historical facts becomes even more important.

Relatedly, psychiatrists and psychologists are notoriously "slippery" witnesses, and it is difficult to fit their opinions into objective criteria. Some familiarity with the American Psychiatric Association's *Diagnostic and Statistical Manual* (*DSM-5*) and with psychological testing is helpful and, in some cases, necessary. However, in the vast majority of everyday cross-examinations in civil cases, the scientific cross-examination based on the *DSM* or testing is limited. Nonetheless, I have included several examples of *DSM* and psychological testing cross-examinations.

ACKNOWLEDGMENTS

I want to thank my law firm, Vorys, Sater, Seymour and Pease, LLP, for the training and support. Many of my partners' efforts are included in these pages. Robert Minor and Carl Smallwood have provided particularly elegant examples of cross-examination. Michael Thomas has provided helpful substantive and editorial contributions. My assistant Bonitta Fowler bore the brunt of the redrafting process with her usual patience and good humor.

I want to thank Michael R. Vilensky, who assisted in reviewing the Common Psychological Concepts and the Glossary of Common Psychological Terms to make those sections more consistent with the recent changes in terminology.

Finally, I want to thank my wife, Carol, and our children, Melanie, Josh, and Joanna, for their support and encouragement.

CHAPTER 1

INTRODUCTION

"I wished by treating Psychology as a natural science, to help her become one."

—William James, *Collected Essays and Reviews* (1920)

1.1 Psychological Testimony Is Different from Other Medical Testimony

Psychological testimony is "slippery," because the vast majority of such testimony is based on information given by the patient. This is particularly true of testimony by psychiatrists, who traditionally do very little testing. Self-reported patient histories are notoriously inaccurate and slanted by the patient in the clinical setting. In the litigation setting, that distortion of patient history is magnified. The goal of litigation is to win; winning usually means some form of compensation or benefit. In psychological terms, this is called "secondary gain," and it further distorts an already difficult factual search in the litigation.

In some cases, psychological testing is administered. Psychological testing is unlike medical testing, in which most tests are objective in the sense that they are laboratory tests unaffected by the efforts of the patient. The patient cannot change a whole blood cell count or a cholesterol number on the day the blood is drawn. Admittedly, some medical testing, such as pulmonary function tests (blowing into a tube), are "effort dependent." Physicians have methods and observational techniques to ensure that effort is made or lack of effort is noted. Laboratories have standardized procedures, which have been well established over time.

Psychological testing is different, although many psychologists might disagree. Almost all of it is effort dependent. How a patient answers questions on a personality scale test, such as the Minnesota Multiphasic Personality Inventory (MMPI), is entirely up to the patient. Although safeguards allegedly eliminate those who try to exaggerate or manipulate the testing, the fact remains that the patient's mind shapes the results by writing or speaking its impressions; this is not a blood sample that can be analyzed in a lab. Psychologists cannot lay a brain on the table and analyze it, although certain computed tomography x-rays are beginning to explore that possibility.

Psychological testing has many critics. Unlike blood testing, standardization and even interpretation of results is less advanced because of its subjective nature and the fact that many of the tests are relatively new.[1]

1. E.g., J.N. Butcher, *Personality Assessment from the Nineteenth to the Early Twenty-first Century:*

Psychiatrists and psychologists live in a highly specialized world. They validate emotional symptoms that most laypeople consider trivial and correctable solely by the patient's effort. Many laypeople have a bias against psychological treatment, which they feel is unnecessary and ineffective.[2] Self-help techniques are viewed more positively, but in the litigation setting, the plaintiff is not seeking self-help.

Even in cases where physical injury accompanies or causes psychological damage, the plaintiff's lawyer has a difficult burden. In a case tried in a rural county in Ohio, the plaintiff had lost several fingers in an accident and also claimed a psychological disability. The jurors, who were mostly working farmers, knew many farmers who had lost fingers in farm machinery accidents and, no matter how hard the plaintiff's lawyer tried, he simply could not convince them that such a "minor" injury (in their view) could cause psychological problems. Fair? Probably not. But it is a burden lawyers face in many of these cases. These attitudes make the plaintiff lawyer's task more difficult, because he must prove not only that the psychological problem exists but also that it is worthy of treatment.

The defense lawyer has it somewhat easier, although not many would admit it. Most plaintiff psychological experts will say "the right words" to get the case to the jury, but the bias against psychology is clearly helpful during jury deliberations. Once the case gets to the jury, the results are unpredictable, so the bias is of small comfort to defense trial lawyers. The "right words" usually require the psychological expert to testify about causation. The opinion testimony must include a statement that the psychological condition was "directly and proximately" caused or "substantially aggravated" by the injury or event that is the subject of the litigation.

This seems to be similar to other personal injury cases in which such testimony is necessary. However, the broad theoretical structure of psychology rarely recognizes a clear-cut "proximate cause" based on a single event in adult life (with the exception of post-traumatic stress disorder

---

Past Achievements and Contemporary Challenges, 6 ANN. REV. CLINICAL PSYCHOL. 1–20 (2010); J.M. Wood, H.N. Garb, S.O. Lilienfeld, & M.T. Nezworski, *Clinical Assessment*, 53 ANN. REV. PSYCHOL. 519–43 (2002).

2. World Psychiatric Association, *WPA Guidance on How to Combat Stigmatization of Psychiatry and Psychiatrists*, 9(3) WORLD PSYCHIATRY 131–44 (2010).

[PTSD], which, as its name suggests, requires a traumatic causal event). Rather, the most important causative factors usually are the plaintiff's personality and ability to deal with the psychological stresses of life before the event that gave rise to the litigation.

Many psychiatric theorists, influenced by the Freudian school, believe that neuroses are founded on underlying anxieties existing from childhood. When a plaintiff claims that a psychosis, such as schizophrenia, was caused or aggravated by a physical injury, psychiatric theories are undecided about causation. Theories of causation include genetic predisposition, childhood environment, and dysfunctions in neurotransmitters. Although these theories differ, most recognize that some element of prior personality development is essential in the onset of emotional problems. Freud summarized this view by noting that psychiatrists deal more with scars than with bleeding wounds.[3]

Because of the uncertainty of causation, the plaintiff's history of psychiatric problems must be thoroughly known to the plaintiff's counsel and thoroughly discovered by defense counsel. That discovery is discussed in Chapter 2 (see Section 2.3).

1.2 Approach to Successful Cross-Examination

How does one confront these "slippery" experts? How does the defense lawyer solve the problem of cross-examining an expert whose opinion is based primarily on just talking to the plaintiff? How does a plaintiff's lawyer overcome the bias against psychology and convince a jury through cross-examination that the client has a valid psychological claim worthy of compensation? The answer is by using the tools of discovery and the techniques of cross-examination. For a more complete treatment of these issues, see my prior book (*Cross-Examining Doctors: A Practical Guide*, 2010). However, for purposes of setting the stage for reviewing the transcripts that follow, here is an overview.

You must confront the expert with materials obtained through preparation and discovery. Knowing the basic facts, the chronology of events, and the medical facts is essential, but you must also know psychological

3. L.C. Kolb, Modern Clinical Psychiatry (10th ed. 1982).

concepts and terms. The expert's prior opinions, publications, and qualifications should be ascertained *before* the discovery deposition.

Having those materials is just the beginning. How do you compete with an expert who knows the medical facts and medicine better than you can possibly know it? There are three ways:

1. You will have to obtain facts through discovery that the expert will not have, including conflicting prior medical history that has not been taken into account by the expert.
2. You get to choose which facts to emphasize.
3. Most important, you are permitted to use the techniques of cross-examination.

Those techniques include leading questions, questions with a high probability of a favorable answer, and the ability to confront a witness with materials, such as depositions, medical records, or scientific texts, that compel a favorable answer. The rest is commentary.

The goals of cross-examination are as follows:

- Getting admissions that are helpful to the case
- Discrediting the witness
- Discrediting the witness's testimony
- Getting only what you need for argument

As you review these transcripts, keep these techniques and goals in mind and determine what the lawyers are trying to do. From time to time, I will suggest what techniques and goals are in play.

CHAPTER 2

PREPARATION

"Luck is what happens when preparation meets opportunity."
—Darrell Royal

"If you don't have time to do it right, when will you have time to do it over?"
—John Wooden

"Everyone wants to win, but not everyone is willing to prepare to win."
—Bobby Knight

2.1 COMMON PSYCHOLOGICAL CONCEPTS

Before you can decode the language of psychology and use it in cross-examination, you need a brief overview of psychological concepts. Many of these concepts are in the modern fund of knowledge, but this overview focuses on key concepts and language that you will encounter when cross-examining psychological experts.

When speaking of psychological concepts, trial lawyers are referring to abnormal psychology. Here is a brief history and discussion of core concepts as they relate to the civil trial process. Starting with the most basic terms, *psychology* is "the study of the mind, brain and behavior."[1] *Abnormal psychology* is the "scientific study of abnormal behavior in an effort to describe, predict, explain and change abnormal pattern of functioning."[2]

Attempts to understand abnormal psychology go back to the beginnings of human history. In the Stone Age, about 50,000 years ago, an operation called trephination was used to cut out a section of skull, and it is believed that this procedure was intended to cure psychological problems by releasing evil spirits housed in the skull. This model of abnormal behavior—namely, demonic possession—was the predominant view in early human history. Starting with the classical Greeks, a new model of abnormality asserted that abnormal behavior was not caused by supernatural forces but rather by biological factors. Greek thinkers posited that imbalances of basic fluids in the body, which they called the humors, led to abnormal functioning. This view largely dominated the field until the Enlightenment, when thinkers like John Locke claimed that abnormal behavior was not a function of biology, but rather of psychology. Locke contended that abnormal behavior is caused by irrational patterns of thinking. Since that time, the biological and psychological views of abnormality have jointly dominated thinking about abnormality.

Understandings of the biological bases of abnormal behavior have increased dramatically in the recent past with the advent of better technology to look into the brain, leading to the rise of modern psychiatry. Starting in the mid-20th century, enhanced understanding of chemical

---

1. S.O. LILIENFELD, S.J. LYNN, L.L. NAMY, & N.J. WOOLF, PSYCHOLOGY: FROM INQUIRY TO UNDERSTANDING (2d ed. 2011).

2. R.J. COMER, ABNORMAL PSYCHOLOGY (8th ed. 2014).

processes in the brain led to the development of effective drug treatments, such as antipsychotics and anxiolytics (i.e., drugs that inhibit anxiety).

At the same time, several psychological theories have influenced understandings of abnormal functioning. Sigmund Freud's view that abnormal behavior is based on unconscious conflicts dominated the field for much of the 20th century and continues to inform the conceptualizations of some experts. Later in the 20th century, cognitive and behavioral theories of abnormality, which assert that problematic ways of thinking and behaving lead to abnormal functioning, became quite influential, particularly among psychologists. These theories have led to the development of cognitive and behavioral therapies for many disorders.[3]

The various schools of abnormal psychology are described as follows:

- ***Biological.*** Mental disorders are caused by malfunctioning of biochemical and bioelectrical processes in the brain. This malfunctioning is likely to result from one's genes but can also be caused by viral infections or injuries. Biological treatments include psychotropic medications, psychosurgery, and electroconvulsive therapy. The biological model is the basis for modern clinical psychiatry.
- ***Psychodynamic (also referred to as Psychoanalytic).*** Mental disorders are caused by conflicts between internal forces, which are below the level of consciousness. This theory was developed by Freud but was expanded by later theorists. Early treatments used the technique of free association, in which a patient says anything that comes to mind, to help the patient work through unconscious conflicts. More modern approaches include short-term psychodynamic therapy, which focuses on one specific problem, and relational psychoanalytic therapy, which focuses on the relationship between the therapist and patient. Among clinical psychologists, about 15 percent label themselves as psychodynamic in orientation.
- ***Cognitive-Behavioral.*** Mental disorders are caused by dysfunctional patterns of thinking and behaving. That is, a tendency to draw faulty conclusions and to engage in maladaptive behaviors leads to psychological problems. Cognitive-behavioral therapies thus seek to

3. *Id.*; R. Porter, Madness: A Brief History (2002).

change clients' ways of interpreting the world and behaving in order to improve functioning. Among clinical psychologists, about 40 percent label themselves as cognitive or behavioral in orientation.

- ***Eclectic***. About 30 percent of clinical psychologists label themselves as eclectic in orientation. These psychologists are likely to include a number of schools of psychology in their practices, including cognitive-behavioral and psychodynamic models, as well as other approaches like existential, humanistic, and gestalt therapy.[4]

Finally, it is important to understand the differences among psychiatrists, psychologists, and other professionals, as follows:

- ***Psychiatrists***. Until the mid-20th century, psychiatrists prescribed medical treatments for mental disorders and provided psychotherapy. Today, very few psychiatrists provide psychotherapy; instead, most focus on diagnosing patients and providing biologically based treatments, most commonly drug treatment.
- ***Psychologists***. Clinical psychologists, who generally have a doctorate in clinical psychology, provide psychotherapy, diagnose patients, and administer psychological tests. Neuropsychologists specialize in tests that assess cognitive, perceptual, and motor functions. Some states allow clinical psychologists to prescribe psychotropic medications, although this is quite uncommon.
- ***Other Professionals***. Psychotherapy is also provided by counseling psychologists, school psychologists, marriage and family therapists, and social workers.

2.2 GLOSSARY OF COMMON PSYCHOLOGICAL TERMS

The language of psychology is the key to understanding and cross-examining psychological experts. Each case uses specific psychological terms. You must understand the basic terms *and* the psychological expert's understanding of those terms.

4. Much of this material was gathered from the Comer textbook. The citation for the percentages of clinical psychologists associated with each school is R.S. SHARF, THEORIES OF PSYCHOTHERAPY AND COUNSELING: CONCEPTS AND CASES (5th ed. 2012).

Because psychological issues vary from case to case, the following glossary is primarily useful in understanding the attached transcripts and the psychological experts' understanding of those terms. Again, this is the way it occurs in practice. Therefore, many of these definitions are given by the psychological expert being cross-examined, but there is some supplementation for purposes of completeness. Even though the psychological expert is being cross-examined, he is trying to put his definitions in lay language for the jury, so this is a useful approach to learning for the trial lawyer.

Anxiety

"Anxiety is an unusual level of apprehension or worry which is inconsistent with whatever conditions the person is concerned about." There are several types of anxiety disorders, ranging from Panic Attacks and Social Phobia to Obsessive-Compulsive Disorder and Post-traumatic Stress Disorder (PTSD). Generalized Anxiety Disorder (GAD) is a term you may encounter more frequently. (See definition in this glossary.)

Attention Deficit Disorder (ADHD)

"ADHD is a behavioral diagnosis, and it's made on the basis of behavior in one or more settings that has to do with inattention, distractibility, restlessness, what's termed hyperactivity and an impulsity." The DSM-5 now lists ADHD under neurodevelopmental disorders.

Conversion Disorder

"A conversion disorder arises when there are physical symptoms (such as paralysis) that cannot be confirmed on examination or [by] anatomical distribution of nerves." Formerly known as "hysteria," Freud described the condition as anxiety "converted" into physical symptoms.

Depression

"The patient has gone into a state in which they feel sad and helpless. They lack confidence in their abilities. At times they feel hopeless. They often have difficulty in sleeping. They sometimes have ideas of suicide. They lack the capacity to enjoy pleasure."

Diagnostic and Statistical Manual of Mental Disorders (*DSM*)

A manual published by the American Psychiatric Association and used by many clinicians to characterize psychological diseases. It is an attempt to standardize descriptions of and criteria for diagnosing psychological conditions. It is the "Bible" for categorizing psychological conditions, and it can be useful in some cross-examinations. This manual is presently in its fifth edition (*DSM-5*), which was published in 2013. The manual has been criticized by the profession itself.[5] One severe criticism is that the diagnoses become politicized. For example, homosexuality was previously categorized as a disorder in the *DSM*, but in 1973, under political pressure, the American Psychiatric Association literally "voted" to remove it as a disorder.[6] Whatever the views of the psychiatric community on the issue of homosexuality, the unscientific nature of the decision has been criticized.[7] Although the vast majority of disorders in *DSM-5* are based on scientific proof, some are still subject to the political and social environment of our time.

Dysthymia or Dysthymic Disorder (Depression)

This "is considered to be a neurotic level of depression as opposed to a psychotic level of depression generally, . . . [but] Dysthymic Disorder is not something that goes away when the stress goes away . . . it's become more of a chronic condition."

Generalized Anxiety Disorder (GAD)

GAD refers to "a condition where a person has a number of psychological complaints, muscle tension, symptoms that suggest anxiety." A more compact definition is "an anxiety disorder characterized by chronic free-floating anxiety and such symptoms as tension or sweating or trembling or lightheadedness or irritability that lasts for more than six months."[8]

Mental Status Exam

A mental status exam "is an exam used to determine, in a very general fashion, the intellectual functioning, immediate memory, abstract thinking ability and basic intellectual functioning."

5. *§ 9, Psychiatric Diagnoses: A 60-year Perspective*, 40(11) PSYCHIATRIC NEWS 17.

6. *Homosexuality and Sexual Orientation Disturbance: Proposed Change in DSM-II* 44 (6th Printing POSITION STATEMENT (RETIRED)). APA Document Reference No. 730008.

7. S.A. KIRK & H. KUTCHINS, THE SELLING OF DSM: THE RHETORIC OF SCIENCE IN PSYCHIATRY (1992).

8. *See DSM-5*, 300.02.

Minnesota Multiphasic Personality Inventory (MMPI)

The MMPI "is the most commonly used personality test. . . . This test measures various scales, including the question mark scale, which measures avoidance; the lie or L scale, which measures any attempt to look good to the tester; the F scale, which measures confusion or unusual faults; and the K scale, which measures defensiveness." The L, F, and K scales are usually used together and are helpful in discerning a patient who is attempting to give an "invalid" result. In addition, the MMPI has 10 clinical scales that measure conditions such as depression, paranoia, schizophrenia, etc.[9] The test is designed to determine whether there are "elevated" scales in any of these categories, which are evidence of psychopathology. The test results must be consistent with clinical findings. It does not diagnose a condition but provides evidence of general personality characteristics.

Obsessive-Compulsive Disorder (OCD)

"Obsessive thinking is having a recurrent thought that intrudes in one's mind in which they're unable to control or get out of their thought processes. The compulsive component of that being the urge to carry out that thought."

Organic Brain Syndrome

This describes decreased mental function caused by a medical disease other than a psychiatric illness. It can be caused by trauma as well as other medical conditions, such as strokes.

Paranoid Delusional Disorder

Formerly called paranoid disorder, this refers to an inability to separate reality from imaginings.

Paranoid Schizophrenic

This is a serious psychotic disease wherein the patient misinterprets reality or creates his or her own reality. *DSM-5* eliminated this definition and replaced all Schizophrenia subtypes with a severity scale.

---

9. T.M. Mulroy, *How to Cross Examine a Psychologist in a Custody Case*, 7 Am. J. Fam. L. 65–72 (1993).

Psychopathology

This is a broad term for the study of mental disorder, mental distress, and abnormal behavior.

Psychogenic Pain Disorder (now Somatoform disorder)

A patient with this disorder experiences pain that cannot be verified by normal nerve distribution examination.

Psychosis

This refers to a loss of contact with reality and may include delusions and hallucinations (i.e., living in a fantasy or dream world).

Post-traumatic Stress Syndrome (PTSD)

This is a debilitating anxiety disorder triggered by exposure to trauma, such as combat, disaster, accidents, and physical or sexual assault.

Projective Tests

These include Rorschach inkblots and the Thematic Apperception Test (TAT), which are defined in following entries.

Rorschach (Inkblot)

This is not an objective test, and it cannot be used to make a specific diagnosis of a psychological condition. Outcomes are determined by the skill of the tester and his or her biases.

Thematic Apperception Test (TAT) and Children's Apperception Test (CAT)

These tests are used for overview and consist of 30 black-and-white cards with pictures. There is no accepted scoring method.

Tranquilizers/Diazepam

These drugs are used to treat anxiety.

2.3 DISCOVERY

Effective discovery of psychiatric issues is performed sequentially, and the same sequence should be followed by both plaintiff and defense counsel. First, the medical area should be discovered. Next, the documentary evidence surrounding the medical history—both prior and subsequent to the accident in question—should be collected. Finally, the plaintiff should be extensively interviewed by plaintiff's counsel and thoroughly deposed by defense counsel, based on the medical history. The plaintiff's and defendant's psychiatrists or psychologists should then be deposed.

Over the course of this discovery, the issue that is the real battleground—causation—will become apparent. For example, if the plaintiff had prior psychological issues, then the case may present an aggravation of those issues from the plaintiff's perspective, whereas the defense may argue that the same condition existed before the injury, and the injury was neither causative nor aggravating.

2.4 Discover the Medical Area

A psychiatric claim is usually made on the basis of a definite psychiatric diagnosis. A *Diagnostic and Statistical Manual* (*DSM-5*) classification number is often cited (e.g., 309.81 Post-Traumatic Stress Disorder). Review of the *DSM* will give you the criteria that must be met to make such a diagnosis. A comparison of those criteria with the medical history and deposition of the plaintiff may provide fruitful areas for cross-examination; however, the criteria are often deemed "fulfilled" by the plaintiff's expert, and cross-examination focuses on the strength of the evidence supporting those criteria and on the causation issues.

Separate from the *DSM* criteria, counsel needs to be familiar with the diagnosed disorder. Knowing the difference between neuroses, which are usually treatable conditions from which the patient can recover, and psychoses, which are more severe disorders that are generally less treatable and have less likelihood of recovery, is important. As the previous glossary demonstrates, defining and understanding psychological terms in the case is essential.

Orientation to relevant concepts and terms can be gained from textbooks. Because of the diversity of psychiatric theories, it is difficult to recommend a standard textbook that is appropriate for use in all situations, but Kolb's *Modern Clinical Psychiatry* (10th ed. 1982) is an accepted older text, and *Kaplan and Sadock's Comprehensive Textbook of Psychiatry* (4th ed. 2009) is a more recent one. A useful standard text of abnormal psychology is Comer's *Abnormal Psychology* (8th ed. 2014).

Research in psychological and psychiatric journals related to the particular diagnosis at issue is also recommended. However, these journals tend to be highly specialized and, therefore, less helpful in providing background information. The most helpful method of discovering information about the diagnosis is to talk to a psychiatrist or psychologist. An hour-long consultation with a psychiatrist is extremely useful in obtaining the necessary background, evaluating the claims, and preparing the case.

2.5 Discover Prior and Subsequent Medical Records

Discovery of the plaintiff's history should begin with medical records. All of the plaintiff's medical records from birth to the present should be reviewed.

All Hospital Records, Particularly Outpatient Records (i.e., Emergency Room Visits)

Counsel should note any indications in these records of anxiety symptoms before the incident involved in the lawsuit. Evidence of medical treatment for psychological conditions such as anxiety is an important element in establishing prior psychiatric problems. Also, one should note in the records any family history of significance. Family history is important, because certain psychiatric conditions have a genetic basis.

Records of Psychiatric Hospital Treatment

Do not neglect records of psychiatric treatment obtained in the armed forces. Veterans Administration hospital records often reveal prior psychiatric treatment that was undisclosed by the plaintiff.

Office Records of Treating Physicians

Prior or subsequent treating physicians' notes may contain significant information regarding the plaintiff's psychiatric state. Give particular attention to the types of medication prescribed for the plaintiff before the accident, and determine whether they are given in connection with psychiatric treatment, such as tranquilizers.

Office Records of the Treating Psychiatrist or Psychologist and Any Testifying Expert

Make sure that all records, including underlying data and forms for testing, are obtained. The tests themselves may be helpful in showing the plaintiff's psychiatric status before the accident. For example, a Rorschach (inkblot) test demonstrates the plaintiff's psychiatric personality since the age of eight. Psychiatric problems disclosed by these tests may be proof of preexisting and longstanding psychiatric problems.

In obtaining these records, counsel may encounter significant resistance from older psychiatrists who were trained in the psychoanalytical school and believe that their patient records reflect the psychiatrist's psychological reactions to the patient, and therefore that the privilege is held by the psychiatrist and not by the patient. The attorney must be prepared to meet these objections and make every effort to obtain all medical records.

Nonmedical Records and Investigation

Nonmedical sources can be very useful in revealing the plaintiff's psychiatric history. They may also be used to cross-check information obtained through interrogatories and depositions. Nonmedical sources include court and employment records and interviews of persons who have had contact with the plaintiff, including fellow employees and neighbors of the plaintiff. Useful information may exist in most types of court records. They will reveal prior psychiatric claims and any repetitive pattern by the plaintiff of seeking recovery for psychological illnesses.

Employment records should be checked with an eye toward the plaintiff's ability to cope with life before the accident at issue in the case. Worker's compensation and sickness and accident insurance records may also yield helpful information. Dispensary records at work likewise may show problems with fellow employees or psychological complaints before the accident. Finally, records of prior employers should also be reviewed.

2.6 Discovery Depositions

The defense will take the plaintiff's deposition, and the plaintiff's counsel must prepare the plaintiff for that testimony. In either case, the following areas should be investigated. The preparation by the plaintiff's attorney and by defense counsel for the deposition presents each side with an excellent opportunity to cross-check the medical information. Conflicts can be discovered or explained in the deposition.

Family History

Investigate the plaintiff's family history in detail to obtain psychiatric leads. Note any family history of psychiatric illness or treatment. The discovery of such family history can stimulate further areas of inquiry.

Personal History

Investigate the plaintiff's family relationships, including those with spouses and children, and especially with parents. Unresolved childhood problems with parents may be the original source of psychiatric problems. This information, however, is usually obtained through a treating psychiatrist.

Investigate the plaintiff's work history, employment history, and general ability to cope with life before the accident. In this connection, all of the plaintiff's interpersonal relationships should be investigated, including any problems at school. For some psychiatric claims, the plaintiff's prior sexual problems should be investigated.

Note the plaintiff's age, because this information is important to the psychiatric diagnosis. Certain depressions occur naturally in middle age. Thus, psychiatric problems that a plaintiff attributes to a minor auto accident may in fact be the result of natural aging processes. Furthermore, some age-related organic diseases can cause personality changes. For example, arteriosclerosis in the brain may cause psychiatric problems that are organic rather than functional. These changes in the brain have no causal relationship to the auto accident at issue. Finally, age may be important in developing cross-examination of a plaintiff's expert witness. Statistics show that most hospitalizations for schizophrenia occur between the ages of 25 and 34. Evidence that the plaintiff suffered from schizophrenia during that period is helpful in convincing a jury that the schizophrenia is unrelated, even by way of aggravation, to the involved accident.

Symptoms

Investigate the plaintiff's symptoms. The timeframe in which the symptoms appeared is crucially relevant. Evidence that an emotional disorder developed some six months or a year after the accident is less convincing for a plaintiff than evidence that the symptoms developed immediately.

The specific symptoms in a particular case may also be important. The plaintiff's description of anxiety symptoms at deposition might not fall within the same diagnostic category that the plaintiff's psychiatrist adopted. Psychiatrists often disagree on exact diagnoses, causing considerable problems in these cases, but the disagreements are obvious opportunities for the defense to show that the defense psychiatrist's diagnosis fits the symptoms more accurately than the plaintiff's psychiatrist's diagnosis.

Plaintiff's counsel and defense counsel should each investigate all complaints and symptoms to assist their experts' psychiatric diagnoses. The symptoms discovered may also assist in determining whether a psychiatric claim is real or feigned. For example, malingerers tend to be less specific in their complaints and do not exhibit classic symptoms of their alleged psychiatric illness. In true psychiatric conditions, such as PTSD, patients specifically describe their symptoms.[10]

Investigate the events surrounding any psychiatric episode. Were the reasons the plaintiff sought psychiatric treatment after the accident triggered by the accident? Or were they triggered by the loss of a job, the death of a loved one, or any other events unrelated to the accident involved in the lawsuit.

Finally, attempt to determine how the plaintiff was referred to a psychiatrist. In most psychiatric claims, the referral was precipitated by the plaintiff's attorney, rather than a physician.[11] The fact that a referral is made by a lawyer rather than a doctor can be useful in cross-examination. In fact, the *DSM-5*, in Section V65.2, Malingering, notes that:

---

10. M. Blinder, *The Gentle Art of Malingering*, 6 Trial 57 (Aug.–Sept. 1970).

11. H.C. Modlin, *The Postaccident Anxiety Syndrome: Psychosocial Aspect*, 123 Am. J. Psychiatry 997, 1010 (1967).

Malingering should be strongly suspected if any combination of the following is noted:

Medico-legal context of presentation (e.g.), the person is referred by an attorney to the clinician for examination.[12]

2.7 DISCOVER THE EXPERT

A Physical or Organic Cause?

If a head injury is involved, examination by a neurologist or neurosurgeon, together with electroencephalogram (EEG) and computed tomography (CT) scan testing, can implicate or eliminate organic causes of psychiatric problems.

Investigate Psychiatric History

Neither the plaintiff's counsel nor the defense counsel should leave discovery of the plaintiff's prior and subsequent psychiatric history to the treating, examining, or defense psychiatrists or psychologists. Both plaintiff's counsel and defense counsel can assist their respective examiners with more complete information, because most psychological examinations take only an hour, and full information is difficult to obtain in that time. Cross-checking and verifying information from other sources can increase the expert's credibility and strengthen the case, particularly elements of prior history. Damaging prior history, if known, can often be explained, and thus may not undercut the expert's opinion, but it must be known so that it does not create surprise and uncertainty in the expert witness.

Investigate the Expert

Interrogatories

Interrogatories are overused in almost all litigation. Their use wastes time and increases expense. Interrogatory answers generally yield little information that is ultimately useful at trial. Interrogatories are most useful to locate records, tests, and other documentary information in the possession

12. Note: "Malingering" in the *DSM-5* in Section V65.2 (276.5) is essentially the same form, and this cross-examination is still available.

of a party. Sections 2.4 and 2.5 of this chapter list the general types of information that are usefully sought through interrogatories.

If an expert's report is available or required, obtain that report. This book provides many examples demonstrating the use of such reports. I prefer to obtain the expert's opinions and the bases of those opinions by deposition, but most lawyers also seek them through interrogatories. I generally find that such interrogatory answers are useless and must be explored through deposition anyway.

Other Expert Investigation

Asking your expert about the other side's expert can yield useful cross-examination. Experts, particularly in specialized fields, tend to know each other through professional organizations, or they know someone who does know your opponent's expert. You may find that your expert was actually involved in training programs where the other side's expert was trained. This useful information can be utilized to increase your expert's credibility.

Other areas of outside discovery may include Medical Board or Psychology Board inquiry; American Board of Medical Specialties (ABMS) Directory of Board Certified Specialists; Medline searches, prior depositions, and Internet articles; and local lawyer information. Even standard witness investigation of divorce records, federal court records (tax evasion), and other public records can yield interesting results, as shown in some of the cross-examinations included in this book.

Expert Depositions

Expert deposition discovery is essential for shaping successful cross-examination at trial. The chapters' titles outline the areas of usual discovery in these cases. Chapter 2 of my prior book (*Cross-Examining Doctors: A Practical Guide*, 2010) provides an in-depth approach to discovery depositions. However, obtaining and *preserving* good answers in discovery depositions is the key to successful cross-examination.

2.8 Planning Cross-Examination

Cross-examination techniques have been extensively discussed: starting strong, finishing strong, and not following the sequence of direct. Deciding what sequence to use for cross-examination depends on qualifications, texts, opinions, credibility, and the need to keep it short. Saying those words is not as helpful as it seems, but seeing actual transcripts employing those approaches is instructive. You will see these approaches illustrated throughout the book.

2.9 Phrasing Questions and Techniques

With these "slippery" witnesses, controlling the testimony is crucial. As noted, a leading question is the weapon of choice. But addressing the nonresponsive answer, narrowing the question (not asking "why?"), and rephrasing and pursuing the question to get an answer are also phrasing issues that are discussed in the following transcripts.

The attitude of the cross-examiner, breaking down the testimony into component parts, simplifying the testimony for the jury, accentuating the positive, and eliminating negative testimony are also techniques that are utilized in the transcripts.

In addition, techniques of attacking the basis of an opinion, demonstrating what is ignored in the opinion, attacking ill-chosen words used by the witness, putting the opinion in perspective (especially important in these examinations), and advancing your claims are demonstrated in these transcripts.

In the first part of the book, phrasing and techniques are pointed out; by the end of the book, you will be able to spot the phrasing and techniques on your own.

CHAPTER 3

QUALIFICATIONS

"A learned fool is more foolish than an ignorant one."

—Molière

"Once you put on the cap and gown all you need to do is open your mouth. Whatever nonsense you talk becomes wisdom and all the rubbish, good sense."

—Molière

3.1 Not Psychiatrist but Psychologist
3.2 Not Doing Psychological Testing as Psychiatrist
3.3 Not Board Certified
3.4 Supporting Your Expert's Credentials—Not Fellow of Professional Society, Lack of Publications
3.5 Credibility of the Doctor

Psychiatrics and psychologists are high-status witnesses. One way to attack their credibility is through their qualifications. This includes not only their educational credentials but also their motives for testifying.

3.1 NOT PSYCHIATRIST BUT PSYCHOLOGIST

Treatments by psychologists and psychiatrists often overlap, but there are some areas in which psychologists are the more appropriate practitioners. Psychologists, rather than psychiatrists, do most of the psychological testing (e.g., MMPI). However, psychologists are not physicians and, in most states, cannot prescribe medicine. Here are some approaches to these qualification issues. First, a psychologist:

Q. "Sir, you are not a medical physician, are you?"

A. "That is true."

Q. "You've never been to medical school."

A. "No."

Q. "And not being a doctor, you are not therefore that specialized type of doctor known as a psychiatrist, are you?"

A. "No, I am not."

Q. "Do you render any psychiatric treatment?"

A. "Psychological treatment but not psychiatric treatment."

Q. "Are you on the staff of any hospitals?"

A. "No, I am not."

This approach works well when your expert is a psychiatrist. Note the subtle use of "You are not therefore that specialized type of doctor known as a psychiatrist, are you?", thereby elevating (arguably unfairly) your expert as the specialist in the case. Note also the clever phrasing about not rendering any "psychiatric treatments." In truth, both psychiatrists and psychologists make the types of psychological diagnosis that are at issue here.

Here is the cross-examination of a psychologist on a prescription drug issue, specifically an anti-seizure drug, Dilantin. The testimony involves a parent in a custody dispute:

> Q. "You have already been certified [by the Court] as an expert with regard to psychology, correct?"
>
> A. "Yes."
>
> Q. "And as far as that is concerned, at this point, you did find out that my client Tim has been taking Dilantin, correct?"
>
> A. "Yes."
>
> Q. "And I noticed from your background information that you really do not have any medical training, you have psychological training, correct?"
>
> A. "That's correct."
>
> Q. "With regard to the MMPI tests you administered, are any of these test results influenced by a person taking Dilantin?"
>
> A. "Uh, yes and no. Some studies document certain behavioral changes in individuals on Dilantin."
>
> Q. "Are you aware Dilantin can cause emotional reactions or outbursts?"
>
> A. "I can't say the study, but yes, it sometimes is associated with emotional over-reactivity."

Q. "And you are aware my client Tim requested that the dosage be decreased because of anger outbursts."

A. "Yes."

Q. "Are you aware of scientific studies that find regulating Dilantin will cause any change in emotional reactions in patients?"

A. "I can't cite any specific studies that would say that."

Q. "As a psychologist, can you prescribe Dilantin?"

A. "No."

The lawyer is preparing the jury for his expert, a psychiatrist, who will then testify that it was the Dilantin and not the client's personality (as shown by the MMPI results) that caused the emotional outbursts.

3.2 NOT DOING PSYCHOLOGICAL TESTING AS PSYCHIATRIST

The other side of the coin is that most psychiatrists do not administer certain psychological tests (e.g., MMPI) but rely on psychologists who do. Psychiatrists may assert, however, that they are trained to interpret such tests. If your expert is a psychologist, then a cross-examination can be done emphasizing that psychiatrists do not regularly administer psychological testing:

Q. "I note you have relied on psychological testing done by psychologists."

A. "Yes, that is customary."

Q. "And by 'customary,' do you mean that you normally do not give or grade such psychological tests?"

A. "Correct, but I sometimes interpret them."

Q. "But you have not in this case."

A. "No."

Q. "And other than in your training, you have not studied or given these tests?"

A. "Correct."

Q. "So in this case you must necessarily rely on the psychologist giving the test to properly administer and interpret it."

A. "Yes, that's how it is often done."

Q. "And you have not looked at the underlying testing answers here but relied on the psychologist report."

A. "Yes."

If there are conflicts in the testing interpretation between your psychologist and your opponent's psychologist, then this approach can neutralize some of the psychiatrist's opinions.

Note the incorporation of the word *customary* by the examiner in the question following its use by the deponent. This is sometimes called *looping*[1]—incorporating a word or phrase in an answer into the next question. It heightens interest and smoothes transitions in questioning.

3.3 Not Board Certified

Psychiatrists, like all major medical specialists, have specialty boards that certify them as specialists. The American Board of Medical Specialties

1. *See* H.J. Stern, 2 Trying Cases to Win (1995)

(ABMS) certifies psychiatrists who complete a qualified residency training and pass the appropriate tests. You can check in the ABMS *before* the discovery deposition and determine if the psychiatrist is board certified. Some psychiatrists are not board certified because they choose not to take the exams, because they were not qualified to take them, or because they took them and failed. Whatever the reason, it is a missing credential that can be exploited:

Q. "I take it you were born in Turkey?"

A. "Yes."

Q. "And when did you become a citizen of the United States?"

A. "1994, I believe. I am not quite for sure, I had to wait for a while, you know."

Q. "And you have been practicing medicine in this country since you came here?"

A. "I had my training first."

Q. "You were interning when you came to the United States?"

A. "Yes."

Q. "Okay. Have you ever had occasion to take examinations for certification by the American Board of Psychiatrists?"

A. "No."

Q. "You have not done that?"

A. "No."

Q. "Could you explain to me what Board Certification means?"

A. "Board Certification, if you want to be a member of a—well, let's see. I am a member of the American Psychiatric Association. I have all the privileges of the Association you know, provided to general members. When you take Board Examinations you are a Diplomat instead of a general member and you are provided with a certificate and it is good to have, you know, if you are interested in teaching and faculties. But as far as practice of psychiatry is concerned, absolutely no difference. In fact, most board certified psychiatrists are in teaching rather than practicing or half and half, you know."

Q. "Isn't there an examination which must be taken by a person in order to qualify to be a Diplomat of the American Board of Psychiatry?"

A. "Yeah, there is one."

Q. "And this is a several day test which is conducted by others who are Board Certified or by Diplomats of the organization."

A. "By the board, yes, nationwide."

Q. "In any event, you have not done that?"

A. "No, I did not find time in practicing psychiatry."

This is a discovery deposition, so the open-ended question "Could you explain what Board Certification means?" elicits a response that minimizes this credential by arguing that it doesn't limit his practice and that it is only for psychiatrists who want to teach. The latter statement is not true. Your expert can, of course, address these issues. However, this is what happens if only leading questions are used:

Q. "A psychiatrist has the opportunity to become Board Certified in your specialty of psychiatry?"

A. "Yes."

Q. "And Board Certification is a credential you receive by successfully passing a written exam?"

A. "Yes."

Q. "And an oral exam?"

A. "Yes."

Q. "Prepared by your fellow psychiatrists?"

A. "Yes."

Q. "And if you pass the tests you become a diplomat of the American Psychiatric Association?"

A. "Yes."

Q. "If you fail, you are not Board Certified and not a Diplomat?"

A. "Yes."

Q. "You chose not to take those tests?"

A. "Yes."

Q. "You are not a Diplomat of the American Psychiatric Association?"

A. "No, I am not."

Q. "You do not teach psychiatry in a medical school?"

A. "No."

Q. "You are not on a medical school faculty?"

A. "No."

Let the opposing lawyer use redirect to try to minimize the effect of this testimony. If the psychiatrist simply says he or she is not board certified, then make sure you follow up and ask if they took the exam and failed.

3.4 Supporting Your Expert's Credentials—Not Fellow of Professional Society, Lack of Publications

Much of the effort in attacking an expert's credentials, as noted, is to bolster your expert's credentials and show that he or she has what the opposing expert lacks. Here are some examples:

Q. "You are a member of the American Psychiatric Association?"

A. "I am, yes."

Q. "Is it possible to be elevated to a fellow of that organization?"

A. "Yes."

Q. "Are you a fellow?"

A. "I didn't apply for fellowship."

Q. "Are you on the peer review board of the American Psychiatric Association?"

A. "Not that I know, no, I am not."

Q. "Have you ever been an Officer or President of the Neuropsychiatric Association of Central Ohio?"

A. "I was Secretary-Treasurer one time, a number of years ago."

Q. "Were you ever President?"

A. "No, never President."

Note the examiner gave him some wiggle room when expanding the question to "officer" instead of just "president," but the deponent would have probably snuck in the secretary-treasurer comment anyway. Therefore, the follow-up "Were you ever president?" elicits a helpful and almost wistful "No, never president."

In confronting an expert who lacks publications, make the further point that the expert has not published in the specific journals your expert has. If the expert has some publications but they are not in the most prestigious (usually peer-reviewed) journals in which your expert published, ask if the deponent published in those specific journals.

Finally, by talking to your expert and reviewing the opposing expert's credentials and experience, you can develop further areas of cross-examination. Here is an interesting example where the examiner clearly talked to his expert about the opposing expert:

Q. "Doctor, you practice psychiatry now. Did you get interested in that as a result of taking it in medical school? Is that the way you got started?"

A. "No."

Q. "You didn't take psychiatry courses in medical school?"

A. "Well, there are some psychiatric courses, yes."

Q. "Did you take those?"

> Notice the examiner does not take the bait about why the deponent became a psychiatrist but redirects the next question to where he wants to go. He is in control.

A. "Yes, I did."

Q. "Were they of value to you in getting started?"

A. "Essentially."

Q. "And who taught them to you?" Who was the head of the department when you were in medical school?"

> Note, this was a low-risk cross-examination question and lends weight to what follows.

A. "Dwight Palmer was one of the wheels."

Q. "Is Dr. Palmer considered a wheel in psychiatric circles?"

> Note the looping of the term "wheel" from the prior answer.

A. "Indeed he is."

There you have it: The witness testified that your expert is not only his former teacher, but an acknowledged prominent member of the profession.

Many lawyers argue that credentials are not as important as the preparation, appearance, and substantive presentation of the witness. That may be true in many cases, but making qualification distinctions and bolstering your expert's qualifications with respect to the specific issue at hand can be the evidence the jury uses to tip the scale in your favor.

3.5 Credibility of the Doctor

Not Treating

A simple and key fact, which is often overlooked, is that the examining expert on either side is not actually treating the plaintiff. In cases involving psychological issues, the plaintiff is frequently sent to an examining expert who testifies but does not treat. This may be because the plaintiff's examining expert is a professional witness who has been retained solely to produce and support the plaintiff's psychological claim. The lack of treatment reveals this motive. The lack of treatment by the defense's expert creates an inference that the plaintiff's treating expert is more credible and certainly has had more contact with the plaintiff, bolstering his or her diagnosis.

Here are some comparative examples:

Q. "Doctor, you indicated that your specialty is in guidance and counseling?"

A. "Yes."

Q. "Did you give any guidance or counseling to this gentleman?"

A. "No, these examinations are set up only to evaluate the claimant, and I'm not asked or really permitted to give any type of counseling or advice or any type of treatment. I'm only asked to do a simple evaluation."

Q. "I am correct in understanding that your area of specialty is guidance and counseling?"

A. "Well, that's one of my areas which also include hypnosis and psychological testing."

Q. "Did you hypnotize this gentleman?"

A. "No."

Q. "Did you make any inquiries about any hypnosis—?"

A. "No."

Q. "—he may have been through?"

A. "No."

Other than signaling the jurors, who may be suspicious of hypnosis as a valid treatment, the examination gives the witness too much leverage to explain. Leading questions are better:

Q. "Were you employed by Mr. Connelly?"

A. "Mr. Connelly?"

Q. "Do you know who Mr. Connelly is?"

A. "Chris Connelly?"

Q. "Yes."

A. "Employed by him?"

Q. "Yes."

A. "No."

Q. "He is not your patient?"

A. "No, no, I see."

Q. "You have not treated him?"

A. "No."

Q. "You were employed by the attorney to give an opinion on two occasions here?"

A. "Yes."

Q. "You have seen him twice?"

A. "Twice."

Q. "In either of those examinations did you find what treatment Mr. Connelly has had for his, what you described as his condition of anxiety?"

A. "He hadn't had any formal psychiatric treatment when I had him under my care."

Q. "Well, you didn't have him under your care ever, did you?"

A. "I mean, I examined him at this time."

Q. "You haven't done anything for him?"

A. "What?"

Q. "You haven't done anything for him; have you?"

A. "I examined him."

Q. "Well, did you prescribe any treatment?"

A. "No, I wasn't asked to."

Q. "You haven't done anything to help him with his condition."

A. "I wasn't asked to."

This is a bit more aggressive, leading, and effective. Finally, the following is a clean transcript approach:

Q. "In your practice as a psychiatrist, you see mentally ill people, not well people; is that right?"

A. "That's right."

Q. "Did you render any treatment to Mr. Broz of a psychiatric nature?"

A. "No, sir."

Q. "Did you render any treatment of any kind?"

A. "No, sir."

Q. "Did you offer to render any treatment of him of a psychiatric nature?"

A. "No."

Q. "You only saw him because his lawyers sent him to you?"

A. "That's right."

Payment

The fact that an expert is paid and is not treating the patient gives rise to inquiries about the fee for testifying, with the implication that the opinion is purchased.[2] Sometimes the expert falls for the old trap:

Q. "How much are you being paid for your opinion?"

A. "$2,500."

Good preparation by the opponent will ensure this expert response:

2. See Cross-Examining Doctors: A Practical Guide (2d ed. 2010), for a more complete treatment of this issue.

A. "I am not being paid for my opinion. My opinion is my own, no matter who pays me. I am being paid for the time I spent reviewing the file, examining the patient, and writing my opinion."

The most useful and successful approach is to uncover the relationship between the expert and the referring lawyer. This will be demonstrated in the opening cross-examination in Section 10.2, How it Looks at Trial.

Credibility of Doctor's Opinion

Many of the cross-examinations in this book involve attacking the credibility of the expert's opinion. However, sometimes an expert discloses opinions that are fatal to his or her general credibility:

Recross-Examination

Q. "Doctor, isn't it true that while we were off the record marking the exhibit . . . that you volunteered the statement that you felt it was impossible to not develop psychiatric disability if you have a serious back injury."

Mr. Ridgley: "I would like to put on the record that the discussion had taken place off the record and had nothing to do with this case. I think Mr. Herrold is trying to take—I don't know what—some undue advantage over this private discussion that was had."

Q. "Would you just answer my question?"

A. "I made that statement, yes."

Q. "You volunteered it, didn't you?"

A. "Yes."

Q. "You believe it to be true?"

A. "Absolutely."

This general opinion by the psychiatrist is contrary to most jurors' experience and undermines any claim of credibility.

Sometimes you are fortunate enough to discover an expert who changed his or her opinion, and you can imply a bias in favor of the lawyer who retained the expert. Here, a changed opinion was discovered during the deposition by reviewing the doctor's file and determining different note-taking. Setting the stage is important:

Q. "Your first examination here and your second examination were not examinations for treatment, is that correct?"

A. "That is correct, yes."

Q. "And you prescribed no treatment or drugs in connection with either of those?"

A. "I didn't. No."

Q. "And you gave no psychiatric therapy?"

A. "I gave no therapy."

Q. "And you were not retained to do that; is that correct?"

A. "That is so, yes."

Q. "And you do many examinations of individual employees or claimants, is that correct?"

A. "I do, yes. I do."

Q. "And you do some for Mr. Bridgman's office?"

A. "Yes."

Q. "And you do many for other offices in town?"

A. "I think that is true, yes."

Q. "And you've given deposition testimony on these matters before?"

A. "Yes."

Q. "In fact, you're giving a deposition next week for a claimant also; is that correct?"

A. "I believe so, but I'm not sure. Yes. I think so."

Q. "And you charge for these examinations, don't you?"

A. "Yes, I do."

Q. "And the number of exams that you do during a year make up a part of your income from your medical practice?"

A. "It does, yes."

Q. "And you also charge for giving depositions such as this?"

A. "Yes."

To the extent that there was evidence, the examiner has now set the stage.

Q. "Now doctor, in this case you conducted one examination and then conducted a second examination, is that correct?"

A. "Yes."

Q. "Now, during the first examination you took notes, as is good medical practice?"

A. "Yes."

Q. "Concerning your observations, is that correct?"

A. "That is so, yes."

Q. "And when I asked you earlier in this case for your file on this matter, these notes on second examination were not in the file, is that correct?"

A. "That is so, yes."

Q. "And you had them off to the side?"

A. "Yes."

Q. "Was this second examination at your request?"

A. "No, it wasn't, no."

Q. "This was the request of the attorneys; is that correct?"

A. "Yes."

Q. "And did they write you a letter in connection with this or did they call you up on the phone?"

A. "I think they called me up to ask me—they wrote me a short letter."

Q. "May I see the letter?"

Mr. Bridgman: It is not discoverable. Off the record.

Mr. Radnor: We don't go off the record in this deposition.

Mr. Bridgman: Fine. Stay on the record. You're welcome to see it.

Q. "Now, doctor, Mr. Bridgman wrote you a letter requesting that you re-examine Mrs. Keller in light of Dr. Airey's report, which you have in your file?"

A. "Yes."

Q. "And is it fair to say that the second time you re-examined Mrs. Keller that you obtained substantially more facts about her background than the first time you examined her?"

A. "I believe so, yes."

Q. "All right. We'll get into that . . ."

The implications are that the doctor changed his opinion to help the lawyer's case or took a faulty history during the first examination, or that the plaintiff concealed her history of prior psychiatric treatment.

Later in the deposition, the issue of changed opinion was further highlighted in a more subtle way:

Q. "Doctor, is it fair to say that psychiatry is not an exact science?"

A. "I think so, yes."

Q. "Is it fair to say that psychiatrists disagree?"

A. "I think so. I would have to say that, yes."

Q. "Is it fair to say that there are many different theories in psychiatry in different schools?"

A. "Yes."

Q. "Are you wise enough to know if the theories of personality, the causes of psychological problems which you think are right today will be right tomorrow?"

A. "I hope that as time goes on that we'll advance, and I suppose changes probably will take place. Sometimes the same things are called by different names."

Note the "is it fair?" phrasing, which doctors read as "is it possible?" in some contexts but juries simply ignore and read as surplus words. Do not overuse the phrasing, but you can use it to get a clean transcript answer because it generally generates less argument since the witness wants to "appear fair."

Q. "Doctor, have you ever been wrong?"

A. "Certainly."

It is difficult for the doctor to quibble with these last two questions without appearing pompous or arrogant. These questions may be fairly asked of any medical or scientific expert, but they are especially apt for psychiatrists and psychologists, because they practice a relatively young profession, and the general public has some prejudices against them.[3]

3. See Introduction 1.1 and footnote 4.

CHAPTER 4

CREDIBILITY OF THE PARTY

"Being entirely honest with oneself is a good exercise."

—Sigmund Freud, *Origins of Psychoanalysis*

Letter to Fleiss [October 15, 1897]

4.1 Embellishing Symptoms

In psychological claims, the credibility of the party is always at issue, because history and symptoms, for the most part, come out of the plaintiff's mouth. Conflicts in history (Chapter 5) and embellishing symptoms is the battleground for these cases.

Here is an example:

Q. "You found that he was embellishing complaints above what you would expect the normal person to embellish or build up what he was telling you, didn't he?"

A. "Yeah, his embellishment was judged from normal to extensive."

Q. "In other words, more than you would expect?"

A. "Individuals who demonstrate these psychogenic conditions sometimes have a tendency to, as I said earlier, be dramatic, exaggerated, perhaps overembellish."

Q. "Doctor, as I understand it, a large portion of your evaluation of this man was based on the history he gave you?"

A. "Well, certainly the history is very important . . ."

Q. "And included in the history on which you relied was your statement that he had . . . more than average physical complaints?"

A. "Yes, his physical complaints, right, were presented, and like I said, in a rather dramatic and exaggerated fashion."

The doctor attempts to make the embellishments and drama part of the psychological condition. However, the jury may logically read that as the plaintiff promoting his case. One way to make sure it is so read occurred later in this testimony, highlighting the plaintiff's somewhat unattractive personality:

Q. "Now, you indicated that you didn't find this gentleman to be psychotic?"

A. "That is true."

Q. "And psychosis is a mental illness?"

A. "A very severe form where one becomes entrapped in a fantasy world and daydreams and may be hearing voices, seeing things, having delusions, etc."

Q. "And he didn't have that?"

A. "No."

Q. "What you found him to be was an immature person?"

A. "Yes, the Rorschach [Note: This is the inkblot test that determines personality from an early date, so necessarily before the incident in question] suggested that the personality structure was immature with problems in need fulfillment and tendencies toward impulsivity."

Q. "Now, you found that he had an overwillingness to emit pain behavior?"

A. "Yes."

Q. "In other words, he wanted to complain more than he had reason to?"

A. "His presentation of physical complaints would be more severe than the actual physical picture would suggest."

Note that the examiner puts the issues in perspective by eliciting testimony that the plaintiff is not suffering a major problem (psychosis).

In the following excerpt, a party's attempts to promote her case were discovered during the deposition:

Q. "Doctor, I've now had the opportunity to look through your file. Are there any other papers that you had concerning Mrs. Lyons which aren't in here?"

A. "Not that I'm—There were some medical articles which appeared in the newspapers that I did take out that she would bring to me regarding fumes and so forth. I did delete those."

Q. "She was seeking to impress you on how serious her problem was?"

A. "Probably so."

Two things are noteworthy here: (1) Always review the expert's file; and (2) the question "She was seeking to impress you . . . ?" is a good one and low risk. What else could the reason be? Also note that the "Why did she do that?" question is not asked, because the leading question is almost always better to elicit helpful testimony.

4.2 Malingering and Secondary Gain

Embellishing or exaggerating can be a conscious or unconscious action. Malingering is consciously and intentionally faking or exaggerating symptoms for a reward. Secondary gain is the unconscious benefit one receives as a result of a condition or disease, such as not having to work or receiving compensation. Both are very much in play in cases involving psychological conditions:

Q. "In your experience, doctor, a lawsuit tends to prolong a patient's complaints consciously or unconsciously, isn't that correct?"

A. "It may."

Q. "And psychiatrists have a term for this phenomenon, don't they?"

A. "Yes."

Q. "When it's unconscious prolonging of complaints, this phenomenon is called secondary gain, isn't it?"

A. "Yes . . ."

Q. "And when a person prolongs the complaints consciously that would be called malingering, correct?"

A. "Yes."

Q. "Now, doctor isn't it true that some people just don't like their work?"

A. "Quite true."

Q. "And some people would rather not work if they could avoid it?"

A. "Absolutely."

The lawyer has suggested that the plaintiff doesn't like his job and that his psychological claim is a conscious or unconscious way to avoid work, which may be all that is needed to sway a jury.

In the next example, the attorney suggests that the plaintiff is malingering in a conversion disorder case, where the physical symptoms—a loss of feeling in the arm, called hypoesthesia—cannot be confirmed on examination:

Q. "You referred to a stocking-type of hypoesthesia. That is something which the patient has control of, is it not?"

A. "Well, it may be reflexive or preconscious."

Q. "It may be that, and it may be controlled by her, may it not?"

A. "My interpretation was that it was reflexive and preconscious in this case . . ."

Q. "Well, you really didn't answer my question. It is a distinct possibility it can be consciously controlled by her, may it not?"

A. "Speaking in other individuals, in general it may be."

Q. "And the desire for financial gain could be such a motivation for a person to perform that?"

A. "It may be the case in a certain person but not in this case."

Q. "That's a matter of judgment?"

A. "Yes, sir."

Here, the lawyer still makes the desired point despite the witness's resistance. Note the leading questions, the follow-up questions to stay on point, and the ultimate concession that the lawyer's theory is possible—everything you need on cross-examination.

The next example involves a more neutral witness in another conversion case:

Q. "Now, doctor, it's been your experience, has it not, that the fact of a lawsuit tends to prolong a person's physical and even psychological complaints. Is that correct?"

A. "It has been known to do so."

Q. "And you're aware of studies that show that once litigation or trial is resolved, win or lose, the participant improves, correct?"

A. "Yes, that has been reported frequently."

Q. "And is it fair to say that all people have psychological needs?"

A. "Yes, I think so."

Q. "And one of these is sympathy?"

A. "Yes."

Q. "And that people try to obtain sympathy from other people either consciously or unconsciously, is that right?"

A. "Yes."

Q. "And people also try to obtain other benefits?"

A. "Yes."

Q. "And some of these can be money?"

A. "Yes."

Q. "Or attention?"

A: "Yes."

Q. "Now, if people try to obtain these unconsciously, in psychiatry that is called secondary gain?"

A. "Secondary gain, yes."

Q. "And that operates in many situations?"

A. "It does, yes."

Q. "And it may be operating in Mrs. Keller's case, is that correct?"

A. "That is possible."

Q. "And when people consciously try to obtain money or sympathy or attention, that's called malingering?"

A. "Malingering, yes."

Q. "Now, what are the goals of malingering?"

A. "The goals of malingering are to get, consciously and voluntarily, some advantage for themselves."

Q. "Okay. One would be to avoid work?"

A. "Yes."

Q. "To obtain drugs?"

A. "Yes."

Q. "You're aware that Mrs. Keller is not working, are you?"

A. "I am, yes."

Q. "And she is seeking some sort of financial compensation?"

A. "Yes."

Q. "And that she has been on medication?"

A. "Yes."

Q. "Now doctor, one of the things a psychiatrist must distinguish between is malingering and a conversion diagnosis, right?"

A. "Yes, yes."

Q. "And sometimes even good doctors are fooled?"

A. "It is very difficult at times."

Q. "And they treat people with medications for years who are actually malingering?"

A. "That has been known to happen."

Q. "Doctor, one of the things that should raise a suspicion of malingering in the psychiatrist's work is that a lawsuit is involved?"

A. "Yes, particularly if things are not proceeding smoothly in the lawsuit."

Q. "And further suspicion may be raised when a patient is sent by a lawyer instead of referral by a physician?"

A. "I think one always has to consider malingering in the back of one's mind."

Q. "And that is sometimes hard to judge when you don't get all the facts?"

A. "It can be difficult to judge at times, yes."

This is a trial transcript. Such answers cannot be obtained without excellent preparation and skills.

CHAPTER 5

CONFLICTS IN HISTORY

"There is a history in all men's lives."

—William Shakespeare, *Henry IV*

"The first law of the historian is that he shall never dare utter an untruth. The second is that he shall suppress nothing that is true. Moreover, there shall be no suspicion of partiality."

—Marcus Tullus Cicero (106–43 B.C.E.), *De Oratore II*

"That historians should give their own country a break, I grant you; but not so as to state things contrary to fact."

—Polybius (c. 208–c. 126 B.C.E.), *History*

5.1 CENTRAL ISSUE: INACCURATE OR INCOMPLETE HISTORY

All medical practitioners comment, often in their records, as to whether a patient is a "good historian" or "poor historian." This is usually an indication of whether, in the doctor's judgment, the patient has the ability to accurately and completely relate his or her medical or social history. However, when litigation is involved, motives for being a good or poor historian come into play. In psychological claims, the importance of an accurate history is magnified, because it is usually central to the diagnosis. Incomplete or inaccurate histories often change or severely damage the basis of an expert's opinion. In addition to this issue, patients may embellish not only their symptoms but also their history.

Even in the absence of litigation, patients in any medical treatment area underreport such historical facts as the amount of alcohol, drugs, or tobacco they have used in the past. Doctors often automatically compensate for such known underreporting. Discovery of prior medical records will disclose such conflicts.

Begin, if possible, by establishing that the psychologist or psychiatrist is relying on the patient being a good historian:

Q. "You have seen Mr. Stevens on two occasions?"

A. "Yes."

Q. "Okay. The history which was provided to you came from him; is that not correct?"

A. "True, the history that I based my diagnosis on."

Q. "And you of your own independent knowledge don't know the degree to which that history is accurate or inaccurate?"

A. "No, I don't."

Q. "You are taking his word for it?"

A. "Sure."

The next step is to establish what information may not have been reported by the plaintiff:

Q. "Did you inquire of him how he spent his time?"

A. "Yes, uh-huh."

Q. "Did he tell you that he liked to travel and frequently went to Florida and New England?"

A. "No, he did not."

Q. "Did he tell you he liked a lot of traveling?"

A. "Hum-um, no."

Q. "Did he tell you that he was enjoying his life at the present time?"

A. "No, he did not."

Q. "Now, did he give you a history of alcoholism?"

A. "Yes, he did."

Q. "Did he tell you that he had been hospitalized in a state institution at Cambridge because of alcoholism?"

A. "Well, yes and no. He did report a history of alcohol abuse and dependency from age 18 to 40. He did report multiple psychiatric hospitalizations at Cambridge but indicated that was more of a function of a conflict with his ex-wife."

Q. "In other words, he didn't tell you he was in Cambridge because of alcoholism?"

A. "No, he did not specifically state it in that fashion."

Q. "Did he give you a history of any drug dependency?"

A. "No, he did not."

Q. "Did he tell you that he had recently been admitted for drug detoxification?"

A. "No, he did not."

Q. "Did he give a history of any problems with the law?"

A. "He denied any legal history."

Q. "Now, all of those areas, history of alcoholism, which he didn't give, history of drug dependency, which he didn't give, or history of problems with the law would all have been important to you if you had received them, wouldn't they?"

A. "As I stated earlier, the historical data is always very important when attempting to draw conclusions about a specific complaint and what caused this psychological problem."

Several things should be noted. First, cross-examination must be based on and supported by depositions, medical and hospital records, or other external documents. Second, this is probably as far as the lawyer can go with the expert during the cross-examination; the last question and answer and the evidence should be argued in closing argument. This is what happens when the examiner goes a bit further:

Q. "You said on direct examination that history was the most important thing?"

A. "No, I did not. I said history was one of several components used to draw the final opinion."

Q. "A very important portion of your examination?"

A. "It's important. It's not the most important."

If the examiner had stopped, he would have had much more to work with.

Finally, here is an example of a doctor modifying his opinion based on further information and acknowledging the lack of information, thereby weakening his opinion and his credibility:

Q. ". . . would you agree that life experiences affect a person's mental state?"

A. "Yes, very much so."

Q. "And it's important to find out what those experiences are?"

A. "Yes."

Q. "And they're most significant in determining whether there is a psychiatric problem and what the cause of that problem is?"

A. "They're often of great significance."

Q. "And, to put it another way, the history is very important?"

A. "Yes, it is, yes."

Q. "And is it fair to say that in psychiatry, particularly in a problem such as—which we're confronted with today, the diagnosis is based primarily on history?"

A. "I think that is a fair statement, yes."

Q. "As would be the cause?"

A. "Yes."

Q. "And if the historical information is wrong the diagnosis would be wrong?"

A. "It would cause one to reconsider the diagnosis, yes."

Q. "Now, doctor, there's another problem in that in psychiatry you must rely in large part upon the patient for this history, is that correct?"

A. "This is so."

Q. "And also in psychiatry the patients are often not totally reliable, is that correct?"

A. "Yes."

Q. "So diagnosis is a difficult art at best, is that fair?"

A. "I think that's a fair statement, yes."

Q. "Okay. Now, doctor, there would be a way to double-check, of course, the accuracy of a history that you obtain, would there not be?"

A. "There would be, to get objective information from, say, an outsider."

Q. "Or to examine medical records which are the subject of the information the patient gives you?"

A. "Yes, that could be significant."

Q. "Okay. In this case did you examine the medical records at Doctor's Hospital?"

A. "I didn't, no."

Q. "Did you examine the records of the Central Ohio Psychiatric Hospital?"

A. "I didn't, no."

Q. "Did you examine the records of the Youngstown Receiving Hospital?"

A. "No."

Q. "Did you examine the records of the Columbus State Hospital?"

A. "No, I didn't."

Q. "At Mercy Hospital?"

A. "No."

Q. "At Mt. Carmel Hospital?"

A. "No."

Q. "Your opinion in this case, therefore, is based on what she told you and some other information from some other doctor, is that fair?"

A. "Yes."

Q. "Now, doctor, part of your original opinion in this case with respect to a dysthymic or depression disorder was based on the fact that she had no significant prior psychiatric problem, is that fair?"

A. "I don't know where I said that. I was aware that she had psychiatric difficulties—I was aware of that, yes."

Q. "But you in your original opinion in this case, said her depression disorder was a direct and proximate consequence of her back injury, and when you examined her a second time you backed off of that a little?"

A. "I backed off of that on the basis of some more information I obtained, yes."

Q. "And you originally thought that it was a direct cause because you felt that she had not received significant psychiatric care before?"

A. "Yes."

Q. "And now you know that that is not true, is that correct?"

A. "Yes. Some questions did arise on this based on more recent information."

Q. "Okay. Now, by the more recent information, you mean what she told you on the second examination?"

A. "Yes."

Q. "You have no reason to believe that she didn't have that information on the first examination, do you?"

A. "She probably had it, yes."

Q. "Were you aware that she was receiving psychiatric treatment since 1980?"

A. "I wasn't aware that she was receiving it on a regular and continued basis since that time."

Q. "Now, doctor, in your original examination of her you attempted to obtain an accurate history?"

A. "Yes. I did. Yes."

Q. "You did not, however, obtain a history of her tonsillectomy; nor appendectomy; her hernia, her hemorrhoidectomy; her liver, stomach or gall bladder surgeries, did you?"

A. "No, I didn't."

Q. "She did not give you that information, did she?"

A. "No. No."

Q. "And you didn't have that information?"

N. "No, I didn't."

Q. "She did not give you that information?"

A. "No. No."

Q. "And when you wrote in your report that since that time, meaning since her back problems, she had been in and out of the hospital many times, is it fair to assume that you thought it was related to her back problem?"

A. "Yes. The implication was that they were mainly related to her back problem."

Q. "Okay. Do you now know that those were probably incorrect and that they were related to multiple unrelated surgeries?"

A. "She did not provide that information. It appears now they were unrelated to her back."

Q. "And part of the purpose of the second examination was to read Dr. Altman's [the opposing expert] further information he obtained on this patient, is that correct?

A. "That was one reason but also to see if there was any change in her condition."

5.2 PRIOR HISTORY: EXPERT'S OWN REPORT

"Prior history" is a redundant phrase. It is used here to indicate history before the event that is the subject matter of the lawsuit. It is generally most useful to defendants. Prior history is truly significant in both its presence and its absence. Did the doctor record a prior similar injury unrelated to the lawsuit? Did the doctor fail to record a prior similar injury? Either way, there are opportunities for cross-examination.

Prior history is most significant in psychiatric cases, because diagnosis is based primarily, if not solely, on prior history. Here is an example of psychiatric cross-examination using the sole "office record" (a report to the lawyer) to cross-examine:

Q. "Doctor, from the examination you prepared a four-page single-spaced report which I believe we have marked as Exhibit 1; is that correct?"

A. "Yes, sir."

Q. "That report was based on the significant findings and observations which you observed during the course of your examination; is that fair?"

A. "Yes, sir."

Q. "That report is complete and accurate with respect to your findings; is that correct?"

A. "Yes, sir, it is correct and accurate with respect to my findings."

Q. "Are there any significant events not included in Plaintiff's Exhibit 1 that you based your diagnosis on?"

A. "May I examine the document?"

Q. "Please."

A. "No, sir."

Q. "All the significant events are included in Plaintiff's Exhibit 1, your medical examination report; is that right?"

A. "For my clinical diagnosis, right."

Q. "Now, one of the first tasks which you performed during the course of your examination was to get a history from Mr. McCork; is that right?"

A. "Yes, sir."

Q. "And obtaining a complete and accurate history is important to arriving at a proper diagnosis; isn't that correct?"

A. "Yes, sir."

Q. "The history which you received was based entirely on what Mr. McCork told you; is that correct?"

A. "Yes, sir."

Q. "You had to rely on him to give you the complete and accurate history; is that right?"

A. "Yes, sir, I did so rely."

Q. "Now, on page 2 of Exhibit 1 you note, and I will quote, 'Memory was poor for recent as well as intermediate and remote events'; is that correct?"

A. "Yes, sir, that is correct."

Q. "That was your observation as a result of your examination?"

A. "Yes, sir."

Q. "On page 2 of your report you also noted, and I will quote, 'He was incapable of active reproduction of memories, and passive recollection was accomplished only after considerable effort and difficulty'; is that your statement?"

A. "Yes, sir."

Q. "When you refer to a 'considerable effort and difficulty' are you referring to your efforts to elicit information from the patient?"

A. "This is a gauge of the transference which occurred in terms of his relating the information to me and the countertransference which is the gauge, probably, of my eliciting the information, yes."

Q. "That is to say, it was not very easy to get all of the events out of Mr. McCork when he first entered your office?"

A. "That is correct."

Q. "Although you note that his memory was poor in your report, do you feel that you got a complete and accurate history from Mr. McCork?"

A. "I think he was trying to be as open as possible."

Q. "I appreciate that, doctor; but my question was do you feel that you got a complete and accurate history as a result of what Mr. McCork told you?"

A. "I feel that he was as honest about his feelings as he could be under the circumstances."

Q. "Was there any information which you requested from him which he did not give you?"

A. "Not to my knowledge."

Q. "You were thorough in conducting your examination both of his history and the remainder of your examination; is that correct?"

A. "Yes, sir."

Q. "Would you agree that a patient's physical condition has an impact on his psychological health?"

A. "Yes, sir, I feel there is an aggravation of conditions."

Q. "You did not conduct a physical examination of Mr. McCork, did you, doctor?"

A. "No, sir."

Q. "Would you also agree that a patient's prior medical history, hospitalizations, accidents, diseases, are important to diagnosing emotional conditions or psychological conditions?"

A. "They may be helpful, I don't know that they are absolutely important."

Q. "During the course of your history do you try to elicit as complete a medical history as you possibly can?"

A. "Yes, sir."

Q. "For instance, you elicited that he had been hospitalized at Mercy Hospital at one point, that he had had several treating physicians, and I believe in your reports you mention Drs. Mitzake and Cage; is that correct?"

A. "Yes, sir."

Q. "You did not review medical records from any other hospitalizations which Mr. McCork might have had; is that correct?"

A. "That is correct."

Q. "And you did not consult any of his treating physicians or review their reports; is that correct?"

A. "That is correct."

Q. "Do you know how many times Mr. McCork was hospitalized or for how long a period or for what conditions, with the exception of hospitalizations related to his accident?"

A. "No, sir."

Q. "Now, if there had been hospitalizations for extended periods of time, that would be an important bit of information in completing your medical history; is that fair?"

A. "Yes, sir."

Q. "And it would also be important to know the seriousness of the injury that may have caused that hospitalization or the type of injury that caused the hospitalization to get an impression about the impact on their psychological make-up; is that fair?"

A. "Yes, sir."

Q. "That is because events which caused prolonged hospitalization can lead to anxiety and depression; is that correct?"

A. "Yes, sir."

Q. "Now, you were aware that Mr. McCork had been in an auto accident; is that correct?"

A. "This historically was revealed, yes."

Q. "But did you note in your report that he had been in an auto accident; is that fair?"

A. "That is fair."

Q. "You did not report in your report the severity of that auto accident in that the auto accident resulted in a hospitalization which lasted for approximately three full weeks; is that correct?"

A. "That is correct."

Q. "Now, doctor, would you agree that psychiatry is not an exact science?"

A. "Yes, sir, I would have to agree that it is not an exact science."

Q. "And that is due in part to the fact that you rely largely on what the patient tells you about his history and symptoms; is that correct?"

A. "Yes, sir, we must rely on the patients."

Absence of history may suggest other causes. Here is a continuation of the psychiatric cross-examination showing alternative causes and their absence from the doctor's office record:

Q. "There are many emotional problems, factors, which may cause anxiety and depression and occur without trauma; is that correct?"

A. "Generally correct, yes."

Q. "In fact, most anxiety is related to the stresses of everyday life; is that fair?"

A. "In general that is so."

Q. "Now, in addition to stresses which may occur during adolescence, a person's family relationships are also important to his psychological condition; is that correct?"

A. "Yes, sir."

Q. "And a person's inability to maintain stable intimate relationships is an important factor also; is that fair?"

A. "Yes, sir, very important."

Q. “A breakdown in family relationships either between spouses or parent and child is an anxiety-producing cause, isn't it?”

A. “Yes, sir.”

Q. “And a breakdown in family relationships could also cause depression?”

A. “Yes, they may.”

Q. “Now, with respect to Mr. McCork's marital relationship, you don't note, you don't make any mention of Mr. McCork's relationship with his wife at any point in this four-page report, which is marked as Plaintiff's Exhibit 1; is that correct?”

A. “Yes, I don't refer to it specifically.”

Q. “Were you aware with respect to his marital relationship that he was unable to engage in sexual intercourse with this spouse?”

A. “Some marital discord was discussed.”

Q. “Yes, but were you aware that he was totally incapable of engaging in sexual relationships with his spouse?”

A. “That was alleged.”

Q. “That would be an important factor in arriving at your diagnosis; is that correct?”

A. “Yes, sir.”

Q. “And that is because a man's sexual impotence is a source of tension, anxiety, and in many instances depression?”

A. "This may be."

Q. "And with respect to an ability to maintain stable intimate relationships, you do not note anywhere in this four-page report, which is marked as Plaintiff's Exhibit 1, that Mr. McCork's present wife is his third wife, that this is his third marriage; is that correct?"

A. "I do not refer to it specifically."

Q. "There are, however, other causes of anxiety and depression besides auto accidents and marital problems in everyday life; is that correct?"

A. "Yes, sir."

Q. "For instance, severe financial difficulties would be a source of depression or anxiety, is that correct?"

A. "It may be."

Q. "From the history you obtained from Mr. McCork, did you determine that any financial difficulties were present?"

A. "I did not."

Q. "And as a result you didn't note any severe financial difficulties in your report, which is Plaintiff's Exhibit 1; is that correct?"

A. "I did not note such."

Q. "That is because Mr. McCork did not tell you that he had declared bankruptcy as a result of financial difficulties during the mid-'70s; is that correct?"

A. "He did not specifically refer to this."

CHAPTER 6

EXAMINATION

"My sickness is that I'm fascinated by human behavior, by what's underneath the surface, by the worlds inside people."

—Johnny Depp

6.1 MENTAL STATUS EXAMINATION

A standard psychiatric exam in the litigation context is described by one deponent as follows:

> We try to determine first of all, is there a psychological problem present, and if there is, try to see the psychological problem in the context of the longitudinal history of this person. The history in our field is rather lengthy because we have to take into consideration almost the whole life of the individual and as many factors as we can contributing to psychological problems. All is included into the history. Sometimes it is possible. Sometimes it is very difficult. . . .
>
> Then a certain portion—even though it is intertwined with the taking of the history—the questions are geared in such a manner that we gain a good understanding about a person's intellect, his awareness of feeling, perceiving, the way he perceives the world, whether he is in contact with reality, whether he is psychotic or not. If not, we move to more subtle items, such as his neurotic symptoms. . . .

So the intellectual, the emotional and the behavior aspects of the individual are being assessed and based on this data, we try to determine the diagnosis and, if possible, the relationship between the cause and his symptoms . . . to a reasonable medical probability.

We have seen some aspects of cross-examining on a mental status exam as it relates to the plaintiff's history, but other aspects of the exam, including observations by the expert, present additional cross-examination opportunities:

> Q. "So being anxious and nervous does not mean a person has a mental disorder, does it?"
>
> A. "No."
>
> Q. "Now, doctor, there are some objective signs, aren't there, that you can look for to see if a patient is nervous?"
>
> A. "Surely."

Q. "And by objective signs you understand that I mean behavior that you observe as opposed to what a person tells you is wrong with them, do you understand that?"

A. "Yes."

Q. "One of these signs of nervousness would be tremulousness or shaking, wouldn't it?"

A. "Yes."

Q. "Mr. Thomas was not shaking when you examined him, was he?"

A. "No, sir."

Q. "In fact, you specifically noted in your report that there was no tremulousness, didn't you?"

A. "Yes, sir."

Q. "And another objective sign of nervousness would be sweaty palms; wouldn't it?"

A. "Yes."

Q. "Mr. Thomas did not have sweaty palms, did he?"

A. "I note on another psychiatrist's report that there was noted sweaty palms."

Q. "But that's not the answer to my question. Did you note any sweaty palms?"

A. "I did not, no."

Q. "And you didn't record any in your report, did you?"

A. "No, sir."

Q. "And another objective sign of anxiety and nervousness would be flushing or blushing, wouldn't it?"

A. "Yes."

Q. "And you didn't note that Mr. Thomas had either of these conditions, did you?"

A. "No."

Q. "Now, doctor, I believe you testified that you conducted some tests on Mr. Thomas, didn't you?"

A. "Yes."

Q. "You asked him to subtract seven from 100 and to keep subtracting seven, didn't you?"

A. "Yes."

Q. "And he was able to do this, wasn't he?"

A. "Yes."

Q. "And didn't that indicate his attention span was normal?"

A. "It indicated to me that his attention span at that particular moment was normal."

Q. "Now this test is sometimes called 'Serial Sevens'?"

A. "Yes."

Q. "And it tests also for concentration and memory?"

A. "Yes, one test."

Q. "And at the moment you tested him his concentration and memory by this test was normal?"

A. "By this test, yes."

Q. "And, doctor, you also asked questions which indicated that his intellect was normal?"

A. "Yes."

Q. "And, doctor, you also recorded in your report that he was able to answer your questions rapidly and correctly?"

A. "I indicated that, yes."

Q. "And this indicated to you that he was able to think and concentrate, didn't it?"

A. "At that particular time, yes."

Q. "Doctor, Mr. Thomas did not have any hallucinations or delusions, did he?"

A. "No."

Q. "Mr. Thomas was not psychotic?"

A. "No, sir."

Q. "Mr. Thomas was able to cope with the real world?"

A. "Yes."

Q. "Mr. Thomas did not show any signs of organic brain disorder?"

A. "No, sir."

Q. "Doctor, you also in examining Mr. Thomas asked him questions about recent events, didn't you?"

A. "Yes, sir."

Q. "And he was well-informed about recent events?"

A. "Yes, he was."

Q. "And this indicated his memory was good?"

A. "That his memory at least in these areas were good, was good. I think the one area I was alluding to was the war that was going on at the time."

Q. "And he was well informed on that?"

A. "He knew that there was a war going on at that time."

Note the question phrasing with leading and looping techniques. Note that the lawyer gets to "accentuate the positive" using helpful points from the mental status exam. Finally, note that the definitions of various medical and psychiatric terms must be explained for the jury, but they were deleted from this transcript to show the flow and impact of the testimony.

Often symptoms overlap, and this type of cross-examination can be done in an anxiety case or in a depression case. If you determine that some medical examinations were not done, either through consultation with your expert or by comparing other records and reports, you might make that point:

Q. "Doctor, did you perform a physical examination?"

A. "No."

Most psychiatrists would not do so, but remember that they are also physicians.

Q. "There are also other psychiatric or psychological examinations which could have been done at that time, is that correct?"

A. "That is so, yes."

Q. "And you did none of those other exams?"

A. "No, that is so, yes."

6.2 Psychological Testing—MMPI

Psychiatrists can prescribe medicine, but in most states psychologists cannot. There is otherwise a great deal of overlap between the two professions, particularly with regard to psychological testing such as the MMPI (personality tests) or Rorschach testing. There are many available tests, but generally few are used in typical litigation. Some are highly specialized and must be studied in the context of the case to develop useful cross-examination. The MMPI is the most common.

Here is a voir dire of an expert in a custody case where the parent is seeking joint custody. The impact of dilantin on the MMPI testing was noted previously. This brief cross-examination undercuts the use of the test itself:

Q. "And you administered a series of tests to my client Tim?"

A. "Yes, I did."

Q. "I believe the MMPI?"

A. "Yes."

Q. "And I think it was the MMPI-2 actually, correct?"

A. "Yes."

Q. "And isn't it true that the test you administered was not developed for use in custody or domestic court context?"

A. "No it wasn't, but it has been extensively researched and some norms have been developed for custody litigants as opposed to other groups of test takers."

Q. "Now, the MMPI was originally developed using patients and visitors at a particular hospital?"

A. "Yes, in the 1940's in Minnesota. That's the reason for the name."

Q. "And the MMPI-2 used a broader cross-section of people to develop the test?"

A. "Yes."

Q. "But neither of these tests were specifically developed for use in custodial evaluations or parental rights and responsibilities?"

A. "No, they weren't."

Q. "And you've used them in that context, correct?"

A. "Yes."

Q. "Now the MMPI does not tell you whether someone is a 'good parent' but attempts to identify certain personality traits?"

A. "Yes."

The following cross-examination attacks the practice of relying on others to grade the MMPI. Although probably not determinative, it is a point that should be made if the expert did not administer the test:

Q. "The paper in your file entitled 'Roche Psychiatric Service Institute, MMPI Report,' is that the test scoring that this outside agency did of the MMPI test you had him take?"

A. "Yes, that is it, right."

Q. "Did you rely on that report in reaching your diagnosis of him?"

A. "Yes, sir."

Q. "That report formed an important part of your findings on him?"

A. "Reasonably important, yes."

Q. "It was important in reaching your diagnosis of him?"

A. "Yes."

Q. "Do you have the test forms that he filled out here?"

A. "They stay with the agency. That would be totally meaningless for me or for any other person."

Q. "So he filled out the answers here by checking blanks, yes or no?"

A. "Yes, sir."

Q. "Then you sent the paper off to someone?"

A. "Right."

Q. "Then you received this back (indicating paper)?"

A. "Yes, sir."

Q. "You did not check the way they graded his test?"

A. "No."

Q. "You could not, could you?"

A. "No."

Q. "They had to do it?"

A. "Yes."

Q. "You have to rely on them having done it right?"

A. "That's right."

Q. "In arriving at your diagnosis, your reliance on the written grade sheet that came back was a necessity, wasn't it?"

A. "It's just like any doctor would find it important to have laboratory tests and chest x-rays, and whatever test he deems necessary, otherwise he would come to a diagnosis just listening to the heart. We need additional input over and above our personal examination."

Q. "Is the answer to the question I asked you yes or is it no?"

A. "A necessity? I don't know how to interpret the word necessity."

Q. "Let me rephrase it. Did you rely on the report that came back for purposes of your diagnosis?"

A. "Yes, I did."

The MMPI has individual questions that can appear silly and subjective in isolation. Cross-examination is constructed to undermine the authority of the test, even though the psychologist has given and graded the test:

Q. "The two tests you gave him were the Shipley Institute of Living test and the MMPI?"

A. "Yes."

Q. "Now the Shipley Test is not designed to make a diagnosis of a mental condition?"

A. "No."

Q. "It was basically to help you understand if he had the reading and thinking skills to take the MMPI?"

A. "Yes, it's an intelligence test."

Q. "And the results of that test was that he was intelligent enough?"

A. "Yes."

Q. "Okay. Didn't have anything to do with his candor or lack thereof?"

A. "No."

Q. "Now, the MMPI has a test booklet and he is filling in true or false answers?"

A. "Yes."

Q. "Just so we, you know, make clear for the record what you did here, you administered this test to Mr. Canter. You then graph the results of that test on a chart?"

A. "Yes."

Q. "In a nutshell, that's what you did?"

A. "Yes."

Q. "There are some 500 questions?"

A. "566, I believe."

Q. "And I am certainly not going to ask you about 566 questions, but there are a lot of interesting questions here. I mean one of them, I think, is 'Would I like to work as a librarian'?"

A. "Can we go off the record?"

. . .

Q. "Okay, I'm going to ask you if certain questions help you make a diagnosis?"

A. "Okay. This may or may not help. I don't use individual items to do that. I don't, in fact, go back to the booklet at all to see what particular item a person has endorsed in one direction or another."

Q. "Correct. I am just asking if some of these questions are on the test?"

A. "Right."

Q. “One of them says, ‘I think I would like to work as a librarian’?”

A. “That’s correct. It’s on there.”

Q. “One of them says, ‘I would like to be a florist’?”

A. “Yes.”

Q. “One of them says, ‘I like poetry’?”

A. “Yes, you’re picking most of the interest questions.”

Q. “One of them says, ‘I am happy most of the time’?”

A. “Yes.”

Q. “Okay. I don’t want to go through the whole booklet but I just want to give a sample of the kind of questions asked. Is Mr. Canter, or any other person, given a scale on the MMPI for, say, ‘I am happy most of the time’?”

A. “No. No one is given explanations. Only true or false.”

Q. “Okay, but you know some people may feel happy and for others in the same situation may feel pretty horrible?”

A. “Right.”

Q. “And your file contains questions that are labeled ‘critical items’?”

A. “Yes.”

Q. “And you prepared a list of those questions and answers?”

A. "Yes, I did. The computer which scores the test pulls out questions which are critical items because of the way they were answered in a way that raises concern or requires further investigation or indicates some problems."

Q. "Okay. There were five critical items produced by the computer?"

A. "Yes."

Q. "And they are Mr. Canter's answers, right?"

Q. "One of them is 'my sex life is satisfactory' and he said 'false'?"

A. "Right."

Q. "Now, certainly this doesn't make a value judgment as to why his sex life is satisfactory or not?"

A. "No. Just to him it's not satisfactory."

Q. "There'd have to be a minimum for that?"

A. "Correct."

Q. "In answer to 'I'm worried about sex matters,' he said 'true'?"

A. "Yes."

Q. "But it doesn't say how he was worrying or why he was worrying?"

A. "Right. That's correct."

Q. "Did you make further inquiry as to why or the reasons for him being worried about sex?"

A. "No."

Q. "Okay."

A. "That was scored after he was gone."

Q. "And you didn't see him again after that?"

A. "No."

. . .

Q. "One of the things that was listed under critical items was the question 'I have wanderlust and I'm never happy unless I'm roaming or traveling about' and he apparently answered that 'true'. Does that have any meaning to you in the abstract?"

A. "Not anything specific, no—[it] was an isolated item."

Q. "I mean is there anything wrong with having wanderlust?"

A. "No."

Q. "And then he said he 'felt anxiety about someone or something almost all the time' and he said 'true' to that?"

A. "Yes."

Q. "Now, of course the answer to that question, would you agree, does not say what is causing the anxiety?"

A. "Correct."

Q. "That could be normal anxiety or something more?"

A. "Yes. Just the pretense of anxiety."

. . .

Recross-Examination

Q. "Counsel has spent a lot of time looking at your MMPI graph?"

A. "Uh-huh."

Q. "The MMPI does not, wouldn't you agree, make any effort to attribute a cause for any findings?"

A. "That is correct."

Q. "And notwithstanding the validity factors you discussed just now with counsel, the way a person chooses to answer some questions can affect how the best results come out?"

A. "I would say to a limited degree."

Q. "But a person can influence how it comes out?"

A. "In theory yes, but you would pick it up on the validity test which would show exaggerating symptoms or lying and there are two scales; one with lying, the other K scale is much more subtle so even if you were very good at lying, the K scale would pick it up."

Q. "So there are questions that clearly are easy to answer if you want to control the test result and others that are not so easy?"

A. "Yes."

Q. "And the test taker may be able to figure those out?"

A. "Theoretically, but manipulation of the test usually shows up."

Several comments apply here. First, the individual questions look like they can easily be manipulated despite the psychologist's (probably) true statement to the contrary. The manipulation testimony is the least successful here, and the cross-examination should have stopped at the possibility of manipulation.

The lack of scale in regard to one's sex life is humorously portrayed in Woody Allen's movie *Annie Hall*, in which a split screen shows Woody Allen's character "Alvy" and Diane Keaton's character "Annie" seeing their therapists:

> Alvy Singer's Therapist: "How often do you sleep together?"
>
> Annie Hall's Therapist: "Do you have sex often?"
>
> Alvy Singer [lamenting]: "Hardly ever, maybe three times a week."
>
> Annie Hall [annoyed]: "Constantly. I'd say three times a week."

This is suggested in the previous cross-examination but could be more fully explored by the examiner.

Attacks on the MMPI are most successful when cross-examination establishes the fact that it does not point to causation, and then suggests other causes for depression, anxiety, or whatever is at issue by referring to the patient's history.

Although an L scale score indicating an absence of lying or malingering is difficult to rebut, there are cases where that attack is available, particularly using SIMS testing:

> Q. "You made your diagnosis of major depression based on your initial clinical interview and the MMPI?"
>
> A. "Yes."
>
> Q. "Now doctor, you did not perform a SIMS, or Structured Inventory of Malingered Symptomology, test on Mr. Landolfi, is that correct?"

A. "I did not, no."

Q. "You have no basis to disagree with the results of that test performed by Dr. Howard?"

A. "I can tell you he often performs that test and I can understand to do it to determine someone's test taking abilities and to cross-check the MMPI."

Q. "Again, you have no basis to dispute the validity?"

A. "I am not going to answer that. No, I have no basis, I can say there's a fair amount of research on SIMS and I don't see a SIMS score not suggestive of malingering."

Q. "Well doctor, isn't it fair that a clinician may undertake that test not only to cross-check the MMPI but because there is a suspicion of malingering?"

A. "I think that's fair."

Q. "And that might possibly account for the high percentage of positive results showing malingering?"

A. "It could or it could be the structure of the test."

Q. "Anyway, you have no basis to find the SIMS test was incorrectly performed by Dr. Howard?"

A. "Correct."

Q. "Or incorrectly interpreted by him?"

A. "Based on, I'm sure, what the manual about the SIMS test says, correct."

Q. "And you said earlier you performed the MMPI-2?"

A. "Yes."

Q. "And the test was valid and interpretable?"

A. "Yes."

Q. "Doctor, you specifically found, and please refer to your notes, that Mr. Landolfi's T score on the F scale was 79, and his T score on the K scale was less than 30, correct?"

A. "Right."

Q. "Isn't it true that a discrepancy like that is suggestive of consciously trying to exaggerate symptoms?"

A. "I think there can be different interpretations of that. That could be one interpretation. Another would be a plea for help, a plea for someone to understand the pain I'm going through, the stress. So yes, there are alternative explanations."

Q. "And in your November report on page 3 you state 'one might initially make the assumption that based on the discrepancy of Mr. Landolfi's F and K scales there was a conscious attempt to exaggerate his problems in an effort to enhance his case' although you suggested other possibilities could be argued, this was one of your findings with respect to the MMPI results?"

A. "Uh-huh, uh-huh. You didn't read the second part because that describes what I just said."

Q. "Fair enough."

A. "Okay."

The doctor is resistant, but his acknowledgment of the possibility that there is malingering, coupled with your own expert's testimony, will provide a strong argument for closing argument.

Finally, here is an example of using the MMPI test offensively. The cross-examination involves alleged sexual harassment and retaliation by a supervisor. The plaintiff claimed that the supervisor made repeated sexual advances, which were rebuffed, and that her supervisor therefore gave her bad performance reviews. The defendant company maintained that the plaintiff was "making this stuff up" and that no sexual harassment or retaliation occurred. Plaintiff underwent an MMPI to support her post-traumatic stress disorder (PTSD) claim, but the results supported the defendant's theory of the case—that harassment did not occur and the plaintiff either intentionally or delusionally fabricated the incidents.

The plaintiff's expert psychologist was her strong advocate, so tight control was maintained by using textbook support (Graham's MMPI text) and the *Diagnostic and Statistical Manual* (*DSM*), which the expert had acknowledged as authoritative:

Q. "You give tests to patients to help you diagnose them?"

A. "Yes."

Q. "One test you gave to Ms. Smith was the MMPI?"

A. "Yes."

Q. "And it is a test that discloses a person's personality?"

A. "Partly, yes."

Q. "And the *DSM* which you've acknowledged as your 'bible' defines personality as: 'Enduring patterns of perceiving, relating to and thinking about the environment and oneself.' [*DSM-5*, Glossary of Technical Terms, p. 826]

A. "Yes."

Q. "And 'enduring patterns' are in part genetically inherited from parents?"

A. "Yes."

Q. "And part of enduring patterns of personality are influenced as you said by family and upbringing?"

A. "Yes."

. . .

Q. "I want to ask about how the MMPI personality inventory works to explore personality?"

A. "Okay."

. . .

Q. "The questions are graded on a variety of scales?"

A. "Uh-huh."

Q. "And the scales have names related to various personality traits?"

A. "Correct, such as depression and schizophrenia."

Q. "And the answers are compared to how normal people and certain people with those problems answer the same question?"

A. "Correct."

Q. "It is a tool to assess basic personality and you consider it authoritative?"

A. "Yes and yes."

Q. "Dr. Butcher and his text [defendant's expert and author of the text *MMPI-2: A Practitioner's Guide*] you consider authoritative?"

A. "Yes, along with others who might disagree."

Q. "Let's go back to Ms. Smith's scores."

. . .

The relevant T-scores for Ms. Smith were as follows:

	HS (Hysteria)	**Hy (Hypochondriasis)**	**Pa (Paranoia)**
T-score [percentage of population who have less of that personality trait]	87	82	85

Q. "So the T-score of 50 is a midrange score?"

A. "Yes, you would be in the middle."

Q. "And more scores are grouped around this midrange?"

A. "Sure."

Q. "And anything above 70 is cause for concern?"

A. "Yes, only a small percentage have those results and scores in that range have clinical significance."

Q. "And Ms. Smith has several high scores?"

A. "Yes, on scales 1, 3, and 6."

Q. "Scale 1—Hs is hysteria?"

A. "Yes. She has a T-score of 87."

Q. "And that is a very high score?"

A. "Well, it is a high score."

Q. "Do you recall in your deposition you acknowledged John Graham and his book [*MMPI-2: Assessing Personality and Psychopathology*, 2006] as being authoritative?"

A. "I don't recall specially but I agree."

Q. "And Graham says any score over 80 is 'very high'?"

A. "Uh-huh."

Q. "And Graham describes personality attributes for such high scorers?"

A. "Uh-huh."

Q. "They tend to be selfish and self-centered?"

A. "His description, yes."

Q. "Cynical and dissatisfied?"

A. "Yes."

Q. "Demanding and critical of others?"

A. "Okay."

. . .

Q. "And Graham says these people are immature and self-centered?"

A. "Yes, part of his description."

Q. "And they use devious means to get the attention they crave?"

A. "Yes."

Q. "And Graham says such people 'act in a sexual or aggressive manner'?"

A. "He says they 'occasionally' do that."

Q. "Okay. And when confronted with this behavior they act surprised or feel persecuted?"

A. "Yes, he says that."

Q. "And [they have] problems with authority figures?"

A. "Yes."

Q. "And react to stress and avoiding responsibility through the development of physical symptoms?"

A. "They can, but not always."

Q. "Ms. Smith often reports to you suffering physical symptoms in response to stress?"

A. "On occasion."

Q. "The next high score is Scale 6, Pa, Paranoia?"

A. "Yes."

Q. "And you described such a paranoia scale as people who have delusions of persecution, among other things?"

A. "Yes."

Q. "Ms. Smith's score is well above the 70 cutoff?"

A. "Yes, 85."

Q. "A delusion is the false belief one is being harassed or conspired against?"

A. "That's part of the definition."

Q. "Well, isn't it the definition in the *DSM*?"

A. "Well, it is part of the definition of a persecutory delusion."

Q. "Okay, Ms. Smith described to you her feelings that she was being persecuted?"

A. "Yes."

The high MMPI scores support the defendants' arguments that the plaintiff's personality is ripe to create delusional and false charges, misperceptions, and manipulations. It further shows her in a poor light, to say the least.

CHAPTER 7

STANDARD PSYCHOLOGICAL FACTS

"Everyone is entitled to his own opinion, but not to his own facts."

—Daniel Patrick Moynihan

Every case has a set of standard psychological facts. Those of a general nature have already been covered and include such facts as: (1) experts rely on what their patients tell them; (2) their diagnoses are based on the patient's self-reports; (3) it is good medical practice to take an accurate history; (4) psychiatry and psychology are not exact sciences; (5) experts often disagree; (6) there are different and differing schools and approaches; (7) patients tend to embellish or underreport certain complaints or lifestyle choices (e.g., drinking); and (8) once litigation is resolved, win or lose, the plaintiff improves. Also, it was noted in the previous chapter that the MMPI does not suggest or determine the cause of the personality traits it attempts to identify.

There is no standard list of such facts, but each case presents opportunities in which the cross-examined expert will readily agree and advance your case.

Here are some examples of common diagnoses such as anxiety or depression:

7.1 ANXIETY AND DEPRESSION: MANY CAUSES

Q. "Now, would you agree with the statement that anxiety may occur under any circumstances and it is not restricted to specific situations or objects?"

A. "Yes, in general, anxiety may occur from numerous factors in life. In Mr. DeRousie's case, it was felt that it related to his injury."

Q. "Doctor, I would move to strike that response and ask you again; would you agree with the statement that anxiety may occur under any circumstances and it is not restricted to specific situations or objects?"

A. "Yes. In response to your specific question, yes."

Q. "An important fact, doctor, there are many emotional problems or factors or concerns that an individual may have and which cause anxiety and depression which may occur without trauma, is that correct?"

A. "Yes, sir."

Q. "Point of fact, isn't it fair to say, doctor, that a significant part of the general population's anxiety is related to the stresses of everyday life?"

A. "That is fair."

Causation is difficult to determine for most psychological conditions, except perhaps PTSD. An expert may agree with the following statements:

Q. "Doctor, there are many causes for depression, aren't there?"

A. "Yes."

Q. "And in some cases even if it's possible to diagnose a depressive condition, it may not be possible to specifically identify one event which caused the person to have that condition, is that so?"

A. "That could be so."

Of course, the willingness of a jury to accept alternative causes depends on the evidence of other causes, which is addressed in Chapter 9.

7.2 Real Pain, Not Neurotic

Q. "Now, would your opinion change in any way if he had serious injuries to his knee before this injury?"

A. "It depends. How serious?"

Q. "Were you provided any history of his injuring his knee at age 19 falling out of a cherry tree onto a cement walk?"

A. "No."

Q. "Or his knee collapsing under him while playing baseball?"

A. "No."

Q. "Or his knee giving out doing deep knee bends during a physical for the Army?"

A. "No."

. . .

Q. "So you were not made aware of his previous knee injuries, is that a fair statement?

A. "Fair statement."

. . .

Q. "Now, the anxiety you described can be caused by a number of different events or problems in one's life, could it not?"

A. "Yes."

Q. "For example, a person suffering a life-shortening lung disease is probably going to sustain some kind of anxiety?"

A. "Sure, it is possible, yes."

Q. "Some sort of cancer, isn't it likely they might sustain anxiety resulting from the threat to their existence?"

A. "Sure."

Q. "All right. Now, by the same token wouldn't it be likely that a person that had a combination of different bodily diseases be even more susceptible to anxiety?"

A. "Sure."

Q. "You gave Mr. Browning no physical exam?"

A. "Wasn't asked to."

Q. "Doctor, a person with serious physical diseases of various kinds is going to have certain real physical complaints, aches and pains, are they not?"

A. "Sure."

Q. "It isn't imaginary if they have aches and pains?"

A. "Uh-huh."

. . .

Q. "In other words, it is a real feeling a person might have?"

A. "Sure."

Q. "And there is nothing neurotic about feeling pain?"

A. "In both cases it felt real to the person, even if it is only psychological. The difference is when we examine them and don't find any physical basis for the pain, then it is psychosomatic or psychological."

Q. "What I'm saying is if a person has a bad knee he is likely to have real pain?"

A. "Sure."

Q. "That's not imaginary, and it is not neurotic?"

A. "No."

Q. "To have pain?"

A. "Let's not . . ."

Q. "If you have an injured knee and you have pain associated with that injury, that is not a neurotic response to your injury, is it?"

A. "No, it is not. It is a natural response."

7.3 Putting Condition in Perspective

Establishing the fact that the plaintiff is not psychotic, hallucinating, or out of touch with reality was demonstrated in Chapter 6, Section 6.1, Mental Status Examination, because it often arises in the context of the expert's report. Such a cross-examination puts the psychological condition in context and mitigates damages.

7.4 Life Choices Are Not a Diagnosis

Q. "All right. Now, doctor, is it your opinion that anybody who doesn't want to work has a neurosis?"

A. "No, no."

Q. "In other words, a person could not want to work and that wouldn't make them mentally ill, would it?"

A. "Not mentally ill."

. . .

Q. "Would it be a mental disorder to not work if you are getting money from some other source that replaced the money you had earned from working?"

A. "Not necessarily, no."

Q. "Now, if a person was receiving money from a rich uncle and they decided not to work, would that make them have a mental disorder if they decided not to work?"

A. "No. He has a reason not to work."

Q. "And if a person would get benefits or payment from any source to provide them with money in place of money they might earn, would that make them have a mental disorder?"

A. "Not necessarily. He has a reason."

. . .

Q. "Isn't it true that some people just hate what they do and hate their work?"

A. "Yes."

Q. "And would rather do almost anything rather than do work that they are employed to do?"

A. "Yes, sure."

. . .

Q. "People who come to you saying they hate their job, that would not be a mental disorder for those people to quit if someone else gave them money?"

A. "That would be a good reason to quit."

Q. "And therefore, it wouldn't be a result of a mental disorder that they quit work?"

A. "No, it wouldn't."

Q. "Doctor, is laziness a mental disorder?"

A. "Not necessarily."

Q. "I mean, some people are hard working and some people are not, isn't that true?"

A. "Sure."

Q. "And some people are very hard working and some are not?"

A. "Sure."

Q. "And a person who is very hard working may be just as mentally sound as a person who is a little bit on the lazy side?"

A. "Sure."

Of course, you need some indications in the evidence or plaintiff's attitude of laziness, malingering, and secondary gain to effectively use this approach.

7.5 Life Circumstances Are Not a Diagnosis

In the following excerpt, the expert had diagnosed a dysthymic disorder, a neurotic level of depression that persists over time even when the precipitating event goes away, and the expert opines that the dysthymic disorder is directly related to a disabling knee injury. The cross-examiner uses the criteria for diagnosis of dysthymic disorder together with the plaintiff's reported complaints to demonstrate that the plaintiff's life circumstances, some of which are arguably unrelated to his injury, occur in the lives of many people who do not have knee injuries:

Q. "Now, doctor, you were aware that Mr. Thomas has not worked for the last six years?"

A. "Yes."

Q. "And he told you that his daily activities consist of him sitting at home, watching TV and watching the kids, didn't he?"

A. "Yes."

Q. "And he's been doing that for five years?"

A. "Yes."

Q. "And he doesn't have any hobbies to speak of?"

A. "No."

Q. "So he's spending quite a bit of time with his kids, isn't that correct?"

A. "Yes."

Q. "In fact, he's around his children more than most fathers?"

A. "Yes."

Q. "And would it be reasonable to assume that he would become irritable with these children on occasion?"

A. "I would assume so."

Q. "You expect he would yell at them on occasion, wouldn't you, doctor?"

A. "Yes."

Q. "This would be normal, wouldn't it?"

A. "I would consider it so."

Q. "Now, you were also told that during the six years Mr. Thomas was home, his wife has not been working also?"

A. "That was my understanding."

Q. "He's spending a lot of time around his wife?"

A. "That's right."

Q. "In fact, again, he's probably spending more time around his wife than most husbands, isn't he?"

A. "Yes."

Q. "And in that situation would it be unusual for him to get—have bouts of irritability with the spouse?"

A. "Yes."

Q. "In fact, wouldn't you expect him to probably have more fights with his wife than most married couples?"

A. "Yes, I would expect so, since they're around them more frequently, for longer periods of time."

Q. "And this would not be abnormal, would it?"

A. "Again, it would be a matter of degree and what it consisted of and how disturbing it was to the parties involved."

Q. "Now, doctor, considering what Mr. Thomas told you about staying home for six years, being with his wife and children day in and day out, not doing much in the way of activities, you would expect him to get bored at times; wouldn't you?"

A. "I would."

Q. "And you would expect him to let his mind wander and daydream when he had this much time on his hands?"

A. "I would imagine he would do more than the average amount of daydreaming."

Q. "And boredom and daydreaming would be normal in this situation, wouldn't it?"

A. "Yes. When one considers the spans of normal, which can be from here to way over there (indicating)."

Q. "And, doctor, when he is at home with all that time and nothing to do, would you expect him to maybe eat more?"

A. "Again, I expect him to eat more or eat less. You know, it could go either way."

Q. "And, doctor, in Mr. Thomas' situation, sitting around most of the day, not moving around much, not getting much exercise, would you expect that he might not get as tired as someone who works a full day?"

A. "Yes, I would expect he would not get as tired."

Q. "And have trouble sleeping?"

A. "That would be on an intermittent basis."

Q. "And he may be sleeping during the day?"

A. "He may be sleeping during the day."

Q. "And it would not be abnormal if he had trouble sleeping during the night?"

A. "No."

We will revisit this technique in Chapter 9 in the discussion of "Other Causes" for psychological problems.

CHAPTER 8

DSM, TEXTS

Freud's ghost on visiting a psychiatric convention: "My goodness, it was just a theory, I didn't mean it to become an industry."

—*Lovesick*, 1983

8.1 Advantages and Disadvantages of Cross-Examination on *DSM*

As noted, the *Diagnostic and Statistical Manual of Mental Disorders* (*DSM*) is now in its fifth edition and is referred to as the *DSM-5*. Although the controversial nature of the manual has been discussed previously, it does provide a common language that psychological professionals can use to communicate.

As a tool for cross-examination, its uses are heavily dependent on the factual situation presented. As mentioned, experts often can align their examination with the criteria in the *DSM-5* to make them "fit." Cross-examination is most effective if you can identify an alternative diagnosis that also fits.

The following examination suggests that a neck injury sustained in an automobile accident may be the precipitating event causing the conversion disorder (shooting pains in arms), rather than the alleged industrial accident:

Q. "Doctor, what damage he does have is of a physical nature to his neck [auto accident] and his back [industrial accident]?"

A. "Yes, sir."

Q. "And are you familiar with the *DSM* criteria for conversion disorder?"

A. "Yes. I have a copy here."

Q. "And one of those criteria is that the 'symptom is not better explained by another medical . . . disorder'?"

A. "Correct."

Q "And you learned he had a prior neck injury in an auto accident?"

A. "Yes."

Q. "And had several hospitalizations and surgeries for that neck injury?"

A. "Yes."

Q. "Now in the complaints section of your report you noted he had a feeling of electricity running through his arms?"

A. "Yes, I recorded that."

Q. "Is it fair to say that the neck injury would cause such complaints?"

A. "It could."

Q. "And that would be another explanation for those complaints?"

A. "Yes, it could be."

Q. "And those complaints could have been from his auto accident, hospitalization and surgeries to his neck?"

A. "That is possible."

Another tactic is to use the definitions and descriptions in the *DSM* as an offensive weapon. In a continuation of the MMPI cross-examination at the end of Chapter 6 in a sexual harassment claim, the cross-examiner shows the plaintiff in a poor light and supports the defense theory that she is delusional about events that never happened.

Q. "Now, doctor, as we discussed, the *DSM* [at page 819] defines a delusion as 'a false belief based on incorrect inference about external reality that is firmly held despite what almost everyone else believes and despite what constitutes incontrovertible and obvious proof or evidence to the contrary'; am I reading that correctly?"

A. "Yes."

Q. "And a 'persecutory delusion' is defined on the same page of the *DSM* as 'a delusion in which the central theme is that one (or someone to whom one is close) is being attacked, harassed, cheated, persecuted or conspired against'?"

A. "That is the definition."

Q. "Ms. Smith described being persecuted to you a lot, as noted in your records?"

A. "Yes, she did."

Q. "You note in your third visit she had markedly exaggerated fears of men teaming up against her?"

A. "Yes."

Q. "And dreams about men 'running over her'?"

A. "Yes."

. . .

Q. "Now, this report of yours diagnoses her with a personality disorder?"

A. "Yes."

Q. "And the *DSM* classically defines a personality disorder [at page 646] as 'an enduring pattern of inner experience and behavior that deviates markedly from the expectations of the individual's culture'?"

A. "There are alternative definitions, but that is a clinically accepted one."

Q. "And the pattern of such a personality disorder is of 'long duration', and its onset can be traced back to at least adolescence or early adulthood?"

A. "Yes."

Q. "And, if you would agree that would be the case with Ms. Smith?"

A. "Yes."

Q. "And you also diagnosed Ms. Smith as having a 'histrionic personality disorder' as found in 301.50 of the *DSM* [at page 657]?"

A. "Yes, sir."

Q. "And your bible, the *DSM*, goes on to describe this personality as one which someone like Ms. Smith 'feels unappreciated if not the center of attention'?"

A. "Uh-huh."

Q. "That 'draw attention to themselves and may initially charm new acquaintances by their enthusiasm, apparent openness, or flirtatiousness'?"

A. "Yes, that is a diagnostic criteria."

Q. "But 'these qualities' wear thin?"

A. "Yes, they often do."

Q. "And the *DSM* further states 'if they are not the center of attention, they do something dramatic [like] make up stories, create a scene to draw the focus of attention to themselves'?"

A. "Yes."

Q. "And Criterion 2 in 301.50 is that people like Ms. Smith are often inappropriately sexually provocative or seductive?"

A. "Some can be."

Q. "And are 'easily and excessively upset by critical comments'?"

A. "Yes, if they perceive them to be about their appearance."

Q. "And they often consider 'relationships more intimate than they actually are'?"

A. "Often."

When doing a cross-examination with so much text citation, a demonstrative chart or slide will help the jury follow and understand the evidence.

8.2 Psychological Texts Cross-Examination

In the following example, the plaintiff was hospitalized after an auto accident with a neck injury. She became progressively depressed and twice attempted suicide. She was hospitalized three times for psychiatric problems and ultimately diagnosed as schizophrenic. She never returned to work after the accident. Her treating psychiatrist acknowledged her prior psychiatric problems but maintained that the auto accident injury aggravated her schizophrenia. Here are two examples in which textbooks are used to cross-examine her psychiatrist. The first uses such texts to compel a favorable answer:

Q. "Doctor, isn't it true that the critical period in personality development, and in terms of a person who tends to have problems of schizophrenia, is during the period of puberty?"

A. "It is highly debatable, it is a matter of opinion. As many authors as there are, there are that many opinions."

Q. "And you would agree with me, doctor, that psychiatry is not an exact science?"

A. "Yes, I would."

Q. "Do psychiatrists, of necessity, spend a great deal of time in examining work in connection with their field, in an effort to get insight into patients' problems?"

A. "Yes, sir."

Q. "Part of your study, I assume, was examination of such medical textbooks?"

A. "Right."

Q. "Now, doctor, are you familiar with this volume entitled, *Comprehensive Text Book on Psychiatry*, edited by Dr. Alfred Friedman and Dr. Harold Kaplan?"

A. "Yes, I have it in my office."

Q. "I would like to call your attention to page 64, which states: 'Authorities stress the importance of puberty as a critical period in personality development. This emphasis on puberty in fact leads the psychiatrist to the term 'dementia praecox' which was originally defined as 'mental deterioration, beginning at puberty." Do you agree or disagree with that statement?"

A. "I disagree."

Q. "Although you recognize those men as authorities?"

A. "Yes."

Q. "What is the period of puberty, doctor?"

A. "It is the area of positive development, where hormone changes take place and people become aware of sex. It is a biological and psychological change which they undergo and it lasts approximately from one to two years."

Q. "And what are those years, what age?"

A. "Between 11 and 14."

Q. "And those people who do subscribe to that particular theory, are saying that in a person's puberty a foundation is laid for emotional problems that may manifest themselves at a later time?"

A. "Yes."

Q. "Doctor, do you agree with this authority that says, 'childhood and social factors play a major role in the development of schizophrenia'?"

A. "Yes."

Q. "What age was the plaintiff when you hospitalized her?"

A. "26 years old."

Q. "Doctor, isn't that the peak period to be hospitalized for schizophrenia?"

A. “No.”

Q. “What do you say the peak period is?”

A. “I have seen schizophrenics four years old and schizophrenics 50 years old.”

Q. “I am asking what is the peak period, not when you have seen individuals, when is the peak period?”

A. “There is no peak period, I think it is artificial.”

Q. “Now, doctor, I would like to call your attention to page 68 in this same text authority that you recognize: ‘In both sexes, admission rates for schizophrenia are concentrated in the age range from 20 to 40, with the peak occurring in the age group from 25 to 34 years, a nine-year period.’ Do you agree or disagree with that statement in this authority?”

A. “With some reservations, I agree.”

Q. “So with some reservations she was within the nine-year period when persons normally have this condition develop to the point where they have to be hospitalized, isn’t that true?”

A. “Yes.”

Q. “This finding is consistent with findings in earlier studies as well as with recent national census data. Are you aware of that kind of study?”

A. “Yes.”

Q. “So they say, within a period of ages 25 to 34, that is the normal period that they expect people to be hospitalized who have schizophrenia, isn’t that true?”

A. "According to statistics, yes."

Q. "Are you aware that approximately 60 percent of the persons hospitalized [for schizophrenia] at the time this text was written were under 35 years of age?"

A. "Yes, I am aware."

Q. "Now, you mentioned something about a person being much older, are you aware that less than one percent are over a particular age level?"

A. "Yes."

Q. "So when you cited one over fifty years of age you were talking about one percent?"

A. "That would be a fair statement."

The continuation of the examination directly confronts the doctor's opinion. The doctor had testified earlier at trial that "traumatic schizophrenia" is well recognized in the medical literature. In fact, he was sure it was discussed in the *Comprehensive Textbook of Psychiatry*:

Q. "Doctor, in this work *Comprehensive Textbook of Psychiatry*, which has an entire section dealing with schizophrenia, can you point out anywhere in this work, which you recognize, where it says 'injury' is an aggravating factor of the condition of schizophrenia?"

A. "It would take some time to review it, but I could quote."

Q. "I am asking, concerning this authority that you recognize, whether in the entire section dealing with schizophrenia there is a single mention of an instance where injury was a cause or aggravating factor?"

Judge: In order to give the doctor time to review that section, I think perhaps we will take a recess at this time.

Q. "Doctor, did I understand you correctly, when you left the room to confer with your lawyers that you said that you were not going to read this?"

A. "I was pretty upset, I did review it."

Q. "Did you find any reference to trauma or injury as causing schizophrenia?"

A. "It is a fairly voluminous book, I could not find it."

Q. "You could not?"

A. "No."

Q. "You recognize this text, *Comprehensive Textbook of Psychiatry*, and you recognize Dr. Friedman and Dr. Kaplan as both being authorities in the field of psychiatry?"

A. "I do."

Q. "In their work dealing with the psychiatric syndromes, they have written more than 75 pages dealing with the chapter entitled 'Schizophrenic Reaction'?"

A. "Correct."

Q. "Is it also fair to say, do you agree, that there are many persons who have schizophrenia, who are undiagnosed, untreated and are ambulatory?"

A. "True."

Q. "Many people walking around have the condition which is not apparent to other laymen?"

A. "Right."

Q. "There are many causes of schizophrenia, aren't there?"

A. "We don't exactly know the causes."

Q. "But of the factors that are known, do you accept the proposition that many times it is caused by factors developing in a person's childhood?"

A. "Yes, sir."

A young associate's career was riding on the fact that the word "injury" did not appear in that textbook, but technology has made it possible for attorneys to check electronic versions of texts for every reference to key words or phrases that may be the subject of cross-examination.

CHAPTER 9

OPINIONS, CAUSATION

"I pass with relief from the tossing sea of Cause and Theory to the firm ground of Result and Fact."

—Winston Churchill, *The Malakind Field Force* (1898)

"Much learning does not teach understanding."

—Heraclitus (544–483 B.C.E.)

"A vigorous five mile walk will do more good for an unhappy but otherwise healthy adult than all the medicine and psychology in the world."

—Paul Dudley White

9.1 Attacking Opinions
9.2 Possible versus Probable
9.3 Proximate Cause
9.4 Aggravation
9.5 Other Causes
9.6 Defeating the Hypothetical
9.7 Mitigating Damages

9.1 Attacking Opinions

Direct attacks on expert opinions are often disastrous and tend to reinforce the strength of those opinions. Changing anyone's opinion is difficult, but changing the opinion of a committed expert is a true challenge. It is better to obtain incremental admissions based on provable facts. This will lead the jury to conclude that the basis of the expert's opinion is flawed. The expert's education and status as a witness is severely undercut if the cross-examiner chooses to attack the basis of the opinion.

Attacking the basis of the opinion has been touched on in previous cross-examination examples involving misreporting by the plaintiff (Chapter 4), inadequate or incomplete history (Chapter 5), flawed testing (Chapters 6 and 8), and the use of standard psychological facts to place diagnoses in context (Chapter 7). Here are some other examples that attack the basis of the opinion and also attack substantive aspects of the way the opinion has been expressed.

9.2 Possible versus Probable

When there are conflicting diagnoses between experts, a cross-examiner can sometimes get the opposing expert to admit that your expert's diagnosis is at least "possible."

Q. "Now, doctor, you have written in this opinion that either Mr. Lonardo reported less severe and less frequent symptoms to Dr. Howard than he did to you?"

A. "It would appear so."

Q. "Is it fair to say that in that paragraph you are concerned about how accurate the portion of Mr. Lonardo's reporting to Dr. Howard might have been given your concerns over what you see as Mr. Lonardo's deficits in emotional language and expression?"

A. "I did say that."

Q. "Doctor, if Mr. Lonardo has deficits in emotional language and expression, couldn't his reporting to you have been inaccurate on that basis as well?"

A. "Could have been, and I guess that goes back to my point earlier of some of the lack of fluidity of how he described things, and it did require asking for more clarification, explanation."

Q. "So those—so it's fair to say that those deficits could have registered in his reporting to either you or Dr. Howard?"

A. "Certainly, yeah."

Q. "So, would you agree that the depressive neurosis NOS condition diagnosed by Dr. Howard is a possible diagnosis for Mr. Lonardo?"

A. "Well, I might make it as a possible diagnosis but my diagnosis of major depression I believe more accurately describes the intensity of the symptoms. But his is a possible diagnosis. I think I can say that."

Q. "Thank you."

You will never get a committed expert to say your expert's diagnosis is more probable, but getting to "possible" is possible. Of course, the cross-examiner now needs to support the less-severe diagnosis with other evidence and with his expert's testimony in order to convince the jury that the "possible" diagnosis is the correct one.

Here is another example of using the "possible" approach in a shared custody case that was previously discussed in connection with dilantin use (in Section 3.1) and with the MMPI (in Section 6.2):

Q. "Dr. Smallwood, you've made some recommendations through your report that my client Tim have some time with his children, correct?"

A. "Yes."

Q. "You would never put these children in harm's way if you thought that was inappropriate?"

A. "I would never do that."

Q. "So during the time period you recommend for Tim to have with his children, you wouldn't question Tim's judgment?"

A. "Not to the extent that I believed he would put the children in jeopardy."

Q. "Well, we've already established that you would not put the children in harm's way, correct?"

A. "Yes."

Q. "Now, you are also aware that Tim had a psychologist do an analysis?"

A. "Yes."

Q. "And that analysis provides significantly more time for Tim with his children, correct?"

A. "I believe that is true."

Q. "So what we really have here is a difference of opinion as to how much time, not whether Tim should have time?"

Opposing lawyer: "Objection, Your Honor, I don't believe that was the witness' testimony at all."

Tim's lawyer: "I believe it's cross-examination."

Judge: "Overruled, it's cross-examination."

A. "My understanding is that that is one of the issues that remain. Another is that the characteristics of your client might interfere with the shared parenting. So I did not recommend shared parenting."

Q. "And you did not recommend shared parenting because of the difficulty between the parents Tim and Sarah?"

A. "Well, my main focus was on the characteristics of Tim that I felt would undermine a relationship that called for them to collaborate with one another."

Q. "Have you ever been in a situation in these custodial arguments where there hasn't been in-fighting amongst the parties?"

A. "I can't recall one, no."

Q. "It would be normal in custodial arguments for parties to disagree?"

A. "Yes."

Q. "That would be, in fact, normal?"

A. "I think that's normal."

Q. "And there's nothing at this point in time that would indicate that at some future date they could agree, is there?"

A. "Well, I considered when the dust settles from the litigation the tensions from the litigation might dissipate enough for the parties to work together but I didn't see that in this case."

Q. "But it's not out of the realm of possibility but not probable in your opinion?"

A. "Anything is possible, I guess."

Q. "And you're aware Tim's expert indicates that it is probable and therefore we have a difference of opinion as to what you believe compared to what the other expert believes?"

A. "I am aware of that, yes."

A more aggressive expert might seize on that last question to re-argue why his position is more probable. The lawyer in this case followed this part of the cross-examination by addressing items of marital conflict, such as the wife wanting to further her education and work outside the home, which she would be free to do after they divorced. The lawyer then highlighted areas of prior marital agreement, such as religious training, schooling, and extracurricular activities. This would tend to support Tim's expert over the wife's expert and make Tim's expert's opinion more probable on the shared parenting issue.

9.3 Proximate Cause

Here is an approach to cross-examination on proximate cause where the examiner in a workers' compensation case first undercuts the witness's credibility and then effectively eliminates his proximate cause opinion. The case involves a claim that a preexisting psychological condition was aggravated (some states require "substantial" aggravation) by the industrial injury.

Q. "All right, now, you said you have been doing these types of evaluations for the Industrial Commission every week for 7 years, is that correct?"

A. "Yes."

Q. "And if my math is correct that's 7 times 52 or over 350 examinations?"

A. "I would say that's approximately right. I really have no idea."

Q. "Now, in each case where you found an emotional problem, how often have you found that emotional problem was not aggravated by the industrial injury?"

A. "Not often, I would say, but that would be, that would really be more on the rare side."

Q. "All right."

. . .

(Recross-Examination)

Q. "Doctor, I have just one more question. Given the fact that you didn't see Mrs. Cobb until 2005, and that she told you that she had been hospitalized for depression in 1999, a year before this injury, and, as we discussed, she was hospitalized for a suicide attempt some ten years before that, that she had stomach stapling, that she had double abdominal surgery and that she tried to shoot her husband, is there any way when you see her in 2005 that you can tell with any certainty whether her emotional condition is any worse than it would have been had she not suffered the industrial injury in September 2000?"

A. "There's no way that I can say that it would be any worse, that's true."

Usually, a long-winded cross-examination question does not produce such a good result, because the expert will pick apart the pieces of it with which the expert disagrees. Here, however, the expert does not appreciate the legal import of the question. He is, in effect, agreeing that he could not say that her emotional condition was directly and proximately aggravated by her industrial injury.

9.4 Aggravation

Psychological claims are based on aggravation of prior psychological conditions when there is a prior psychological history. The previous example is one approach to dealing with that issue. Here is another, involving alleged aggravation of a preexisting anxiety disorder:

Q. "Did you receive a history of alcoholism?"

A. "Yes."

Q. "But not a history of drug dependency?"

A. "No, he denied that."

Q. "Now if you were told he had a history of drug dependency and had been hospitalized for detoxification, could the alcoholism and drug dependency be a basis of the anxiety condition?"

A. "Well, certainly, as I stated earlier, the presence of either alcohol and/or drug abuse can exacerbate emotional problems such as depression and sometimes anxiety."

Q. "Did you receive a history of automobile accidents?"

A. "No."

Q. "Any history of multiple surgeries?"

A. "Yes."

Q. "If there had been automobile accidents, those could have been the cause for an aggravation of his pre-existing anxiety disorder, isn't that so?"

A. "Depending on the severity of the car accidents, it could be a factor."

Q. "And if he had a number of surgeries, that could be a cause of increased anxiety?"

. . .

A. "Well, surgeries certainly can cause an increase in anxiety or depression."

9.5 Other Causes

Whether you are cross-examining on issues related to the proximate cause or aggravation of emotional problems, the defense is looking for "other causes" like those discussed earlier.

Here are some further examples. The first is similar to the examination concerning absence of prior history or conflicts in history (Chapter 5), which naturally leads to an examination of whether that absent or conflicting history is an alternative cause of the psychological condition or its symptoms.

Q. "Now, if he were hostile, as I think you said he was, that could be just his personality, couldn't it?"

A. "He did, as I noted earlier, demonstrate some hostility, and usually anger or hostility is more a function of personality than it is of neurosis."

Q. "Or the hostility you found or felt could also flow from a drug or alcohol dependency, couldn't it?"

A. "Well, some of them do tend to be hostile or angry but that is a function of their personality as opposed to their alcohol abuse."

Q. "Uh-huh. And I think you noted in your report that he looked sad?"

A. "Yes, I noted that some depression was present, sad facial musculature and reduced mirth response."

Q. "And that could be just personality, couldn't it?"

A. "Well, depression or anxiety usually is not a normal function of the personality."

Q. "There are sad people and there are happy people, aren't there?"

A. "I guess in the layman's sense that's true but when I comment on anxiety and depression I'm suggesting a little bit more beyond the normal variation of a normally happy or sad person."

Q. "Now, doctor, he told you he had a low energy level, he ate a lot, slept poorly, had a poor sex drive and his immediate memory was poor?"

A. "Yes."

Q. "And those could all be the kind of reactions one would have if he was drug dependent, isn't that true?"

A. "Some of those things could be correlated with substance abuse. If he was taking depressants, the energy level would be inhibited, sleep and sex drive could be disrupted, memory could be impaired. It wouldn't necessarily account for a high appetite but could account for some of those other features."

Q. "When you say substance abuse, could that be drugs as well as alcohol?"

A. "Well, from alcohol and some other type of depressant would cause those."

Prior medical condition can be another cause for psychological conditions such as anxiety. Here are the final questions in such an examination:

Q. "Doctor, if a person has a combination of diabetes, arteriosclerotic disease, cardio-vascular disease and, as you say, has sustained at least two heart attacks, aren't those serious medical conditions?"

A. "Yes. True."

Q. "Aren't those the type of serious medical conditions which you previously testified would give one cause to be anxious because it poses a threat to one's life or one's survival?"

A. "Sure."

Sometimes social relationships, family circumstances, and physical attributes can all be used to suggest that it was not the physical injury at issue that caused the psychological condition.

Q. "Would you agree that Ms. Johnson is a very large woman?"

A. "Yes, yes."

Q. "She has a big bone structure, she is fairly tall?"

A. "She is tall, yes."

Q. "Would you agree that psychiatry is not an exact science?"

A. "I certainly would, yes."

Q. "A person's family relationships have an important impact on psychiatric conditions, is that correct?"

A. "Yes. I mean they can influence one's kind of mood and disposition, certainly."

Q. "And marital status or lack of a marital relationship can have an important impact on the psychiatric condition, is that a fair statement?"

A. "I should think so, yes."

Q. "A person's inability to maintain a stable, intimate relationship is an important factor also in evaluating a person's psychiatric health, is that true?"

A. "Yes, that is something that one would take into consideration."

Q. "And a breakdown in family relationships may cause depression, is that fair?"

A. "Yes, that is one cause of depression, yes."

Q. "And age or advancing age can also contribute to depression, is that fair?"

A. "I suppose, yes."

. . .

Q. "Does appearance in some cases contribute to depression?"

A. "Yes, I would think so."

Q. "Does the use of prescription analgesics or pain medication or the use of tranquilizers or sedatives cause or contribute to depression?"

A. “Yes, they can do so.”

Q. “Now, in your report, you note that Betty was not married at the time of your examination, is that correct?”

A. “Yes.”

Q. “Did you note whether she was ever married?”

A. “I don’t think so.”

Q. “She was 51 years old at the time of your examination?”

A. “Yes.”

Q. “And you noted in your report her ‘social activities have slacked off’?”

A. “Yes, that’s a fair statement of what I wrote.”

. . .

Q. “Doctor, in general, is it unusual for a 51-year-old unmarried woman who is fairly large to experience a slackening of her social activities as age advances?”

A. “I would say it is reasonable in general to say that as people get older that their social activities, you know, do alter and slack.”

Q. “Do you know if she had any sex life at the time of your examination?”

A. “I didn’t, no.”

Q. “And you did not inquire?”

A. "No."

Q. "To your knowledge, had she ever had a stable, intimate relationship with a man?"

A. "I couldn't answer that. I don't know."

Q. "Now, there are many causes for depression?"

A. "Yes."

Q. "And in some cases, even if it's possible to diagnose that a person has a depression, it may not be possible to specifically identify one event which caused that person to have that condition, is that fair?"

A. "That is so, yes."

This is a somewhat difficult and risky approach, but if the facts and your expert support this hypothesis, you must explore it as gracefully as possible.

Sometimes the cause of the psychological problem may be the plaintiff's pre-injury psychological makeup:

Q. "Now, he had a history of colitis and chest pains?"

A. "Yes."

Q. "And those preceded the injury in this case?"

A. "I'm assuming yes but don't have the dates."

Q. "Colitis can certainly involve an emotional component?"

A. "Yes, it is thought to."

Q. "And certainly some people who have chest pains without heart or cardiac pathology, that can also be an indication of some sort of psychiatric response to stress?"

A. "Correct."

Q. "So, Mr. Cook presented you with a history of those kinds of problems before the injury?"

A. "Yes. Of course, I can also say that just because he had chest pain or colitis doesn't mean necessarily that he is anxious."

Q. "Well, there could be mental and there could be physical causes of chest pain?"

A. "Right, they're co-existing."

Q. "If it's a physical cause you've probably got some problem in your heart or lungs or circulation and he didn't have that?"

A. "Not to my knowledge . . ."

Q. "So the alternative is that he was probably having a stress induced feeling or symptoms of chest pain?"

A. "I certainly thought that was a possibility."

Here is a more extended cross-examination of other possible causes, which by their sheer number decrease the probability that an injury caused the present psychological problem:

Q. "Now, there are many causes of such things as dysthymic disorder or depressions?"

A. "Yes."

Q. "Not just back injuries cause them, is that correct?"

A. "That's correct, yes. That is so."

Q. "Many people get depressed, is that fair?"

A. "Yes."

Q. "And depression, I believe, is caused by—in terms you used: stresses in life, is that correct?"

A. "Stresses in life, yes, they can be significant in bringing about the onset of a depression."

Q. And these stresses can be both physical or they can be things that happen to people in their personal life, their relationships; is that correct?"

A. "Yes. Such as losses and other occurrences."

Q. "Okay. Interpersonal disruptions?"

A. "Yes."

Q. "Relationships that go bad?"

A. "Yes."

Q. "Now, doctor, in psychiatry when someone usually gets a condition in early adult life, what age are they speaking of?"

A. "I suppose under 30 is conventional."

Q. "Anyone over 30 is moving on?"

A. "Yes."

Q. "A dysthymic disorder is one that usually begins in early life, is that correct?"

A. "People with dysthymic disorders, if you look back and take the history, you discover that they have had episodes in earlier life as well."

Q. "Okay. When Ms. Keller had her back injury she was some 35 years old; is that correct?"

A. "Yes. I think. Yes, that is correct, yes."

. . .

Q. "Now, doctor, physical problems can also bring on depressions?"

A. "That is so, yes."

Q. "And would you agree Ms. Keller had a multitude of physical problems?"

A. "I believe she did have, yes."

Q. "In addition to her back problem; is that correct?"

A. "Yes."

Q. "And, in fairness, it's often difficult to separate out which of those problems are significant?"

A. "Yes."

Q. "Her problems include liver, stomach, gallbladder, hernia, mastectomy and back problems. Which one of those, doctor, would you feel would have the most profound psychological effect on somebody just from an objective standpoint?"

A. "I think it is very difficult to generalize. It depends on the severity of the condition and on the amount of interference that physical disorder would bring, say, in one's mobility to function."

Q. "Now, doctor, is it fair to say that patients following mastectomies do have depressions?"

A. "Some people have quite severe adjustment reactions to mastectomy."

Q. "And do you know when her breast surgeries were performed?"

A. "I can't tell you the date, no."

Q. "Do you know if it was a single or double mastectomy?"

A. "I think she had a double mastectomy, which she told me was nonmalignant."

Q. "Due to a cystic condition?"

A. "Yes, a cystic condition, yes."

Q. "And that based on your training you would expect some psychological impact on her?"

A. "Yes. Yes."

Q. "Is it fair to say that all of the things we've discussed in terms of her physical problems could have a cumulative effect on her?"

A. "I think one could say that, yes."

Q. "Now, doctor, moving on to personal problems or social problems or interpersonal problems which cause stress and lead to depression, are marriage problems one of these?"

A. "Yes."

Q. "And school problems [are] one of these?"

A. "Yes."

Q. "And problems with children?"

A. "Yes."

Q. "And problems with drugs and alcohol?"

A. "Yes."

Q. "And you see these every day in your practice?

A. "Yes."

Q. "And these stresses can cause dysthymic depression?"

A. "Yes, I would say in certain people, yes."

Q. "Are you aware when Ms. Keller was first married?"

A. "I'm not aware of the date, but I do know that she had five marriages and three husbands."

Q. "You did not record that in your first letter report, did you?"

A. "No, I didn't, no."

Q. "Did you learn that subsequently?"

A. "Yes."

Q. "And what you recorded in your first letter report was that she told you she was divorced—or that she was married three times?"

A. "Yes. I think there was a marriage since, between those two times she came to see me."

Q. "So when she saw you there were four marriages. She told you three?"

A. "Yes. I wasn't too sure of the statistics of her marriages, yes."

Q. "Okay. Someone who is married as a teenager, is that a stressful situation for people?"

A. "Sometimes is, yes."

Q. "And if there is a child involved, does that add to the stress?"

A. "Yes, children, yes."

Q. "And does that often lead to depression?"

A. "Well, depending on the child and the child's health and behavior in general."

Q. "It can very well?"

A. "Yes."

Q. "Are you aware of what problems she had in school concerning graduating from high school and being married?"

A. "I was of the opinion that she graduated from high school."

Q. "Did you investigate any problems she had in that regard?"

A. "No, I didn't go into full details."

Q. "Now, does divorce cause stress?"

A. "Yes, certainly."

Q. "In all people?"

A. "They are stressful situations."

Q. "And they can lead to depressions such as dysthymic disorders?"

A. "It can lead to depressions, yes."

Q. "Or major depressions?"

A. "Yes."

Q. "Were you aware of the problems she had with any of her husbands?"

A. "I wasn't aware of the details of the difficulties she had."

Q. "That would have an impact on her psychological make-up, though, wouldn't it?"

A. "That would influence her mental state, yes."

Q. "And the greater the problems, the more likelihood that her mental state would be affected?"

A. "Yes."

Q. "Would you agree that if one of her husbands was an alcoholic that could cause stress and depression in her?"

A. "Yes, it could, yes."

Q. "And if he ran around with women, that could further cause stress and depression?"

A. "Yes."

Q. "And if her children at some point in her life were placed in foster homes, that could cause stress and depression?"

A. "Yes."

Q. "And if her husband was at some time accused of molesting children, that would be upsetting and depressing?"

A. "Certainly, yes."

Q. "And if some of these characteristics, such as running around with women, were true of her present husband, that would also be upsetting and depressing?"

A. "Yes, it would, yes."

Q. "Now, you were aware that when she had a hysterectomy she was upset because she couldn't have any more children?"

A. "Yes."

Q. "And you took that as being true, that that upset her?"

A. "Yes, I assumed it was, yes."

Q. "And you made note that she had not seen very much of her children?"

A. "Yes."

Q. "Did you investigate the reason for that?"

A. "No, I didn't, no."

Q. "And you are not aware of that reason?"

A. "No."

Exploration of other causes can continue in this vein and may include, in modern psychological theory, genetic predisposition. Examinations also can include similar prior symptoms, particularly in conversion cases.

9.6 Defeating the Hypothetical

In modern practice, hypothetical questions are used less often but are still asked. One way to defeat the hypothetical is to show that the facts on which it is based are not in evidence. Another way is to present an alternative hypothetical based on your facts in evidence. Using the last transcript example in Section 9.5, the next questions touch on that alternative hypothetical question technique:

Q. "Doctor, I would like you to assume the information that I've given you in the record concerning her personal life and her physical operations, including her depression. Would it be fair to say that even absent a back injury, you would not be surprised if this woman had dysthymic depression?"

A. "I wouldn't have been surprised, no."

Q. "Is it fair to say that this woman's life has many potential causes for such a problem?"

A. "Yes."

Q. "And is it fair to say that another doctor in this case, Dr. Rockwell, states that Ms. Keller has dysthymic disorder but he does not indicate the cause?"

A. "He mentioned nothing about the cause."

Q. "Would it be fair to say that although Ms. Keller told you many things about her back injury, there were many things she did not tell you?"

A. "Yes, I would say that, yes."

Q. "Have you found in your practice that people blame their problems on things that are not really the cause of their problems?"

A. "People can miscalculate, misjudge. That's possible."

Q. "And, in fact, doctor, a great deal of your therapy would involve giving some people insight as to the real cause of their problems?"

A. "Yes, to help them obtain their own insight."

Similarly, in the second example in Section 9.5, Other Causes, involving social relations and physical attributes as other possible causes of the plaintiff's psychological condition, rather than her shoulder injury, here are some alternate hypotheticals concluding that examination:

Q. "I'd like to ask you a hypothetical question, doctor. I'd like you to assume a 51-year-old woman who is large and tall had a hysterectomy at age 41, is unmarried and has never been married, is living alone with her mother, has noticed a slacking off of her social life and exhibits certain signs of depression. Doctor, based upon these factors alone would it be your opinion that the depression which she exhibits would be attributable to one of those factors?"

A. "I would say it possibly could be."

Q. "And, doctor, if Ms. Johnson presented in your office with the history you took, absent the shoulder injury, would your diagnosis have been that she suffered a depressive neurosis?"

A. "Yes."

Q. "And there is nothing peculiar in this case about a shoulder injury which led to depression? Any serious injury would have been an important contributing factor in her depression, is that correct?"

A. "Yes."

Q. "And if she had presented with a back injury you could have easily attributed her depression to the back injury?"

A. "Yes."

Alternate hypotheticals often do not work with committed advocate experts, and discovery depositions must be used to test whether a favorable answer will be elicited. If not, the better course is to set up the "other causes" and then argue in closing argument that those other causes, without the injury, are the real probable cause.

9.7 Mitigating Damages

Trying to mitigate damages is always a part of any defense cross-examination, whether or not there is a solid defense to liability. Here are some approaches to mitigating damages in psychological claims.

The first two examples demonstrate recovery from or improvement in the psychological condition, coupled with the ability to perform daily tasks. This puts the extent of the psychological problem into a favorable perspective for the jury.

In the following divorce case, involving a serious obsessive-compulsive disorder and depression, the spouse claimed that she is able to work as a nurse only two days per week because of these disorders:

Q. "Doctor, how long will you have to continue to see her, is there any way to know?"

A. "No. I don't know."

Q. "It could end next week?"

A. "I would not expect it to end next week because I think she's chronically depressed now."

Q. "Could it end when this divorce ends, or her situation improves significantly? Isn't a lot of her depression now related to the divorce, and the things she has to deal with in connection with it, and working with lawyers, and decisions she has to make? Isn't that a lot of her problem now, or a lot of her concern?"

A. "That is part of her concern. It's not all of it."

Q. "It's a lot of it, according to those notes from the last sessions that I noticed?"

A. "Yes. The last couple of sessions, as the court date has drawn near, she's been very concerned about it."

Q. "So, when that ends, and is over, then that part of her worry is gone, I take it, it will end?"

A. “Part of her concern and worry, yes.”

. . .

Q. “Doctor, you’ve indicated there has been improvement in her during the period of your treatment. Can you tell us in specifics how she has improved?”

A. “The degree of depression has waxed and waned. She is less depressed at times, she’s less anxious at times, and then at other times she’s more so. The course has not been one of smooth improvement by any means.”

Q. “There’s been no indication to have her even consider hospitalization ever again, I assume?”

A. “No. I don’t believe we’ve had to consider re-hospitalization.”

. . .

Q. “She is an intelligent woman, isn’t she, doctor?”

A. “She’s very bright.”

Q. “And she’s able to assess her own feelings?”

A. “Yes, for the most part.”

Q. “And those descriptions, as far as you know, have been accurate and reliable?”

A. “Yes.”

. . .

Q. "Well, how will you know if she is ever ready to work full time?"

A. "That'll be a matter of clinical judgment."

Q. "And that'll be a matter of her own will, and her own desire, too, won't it?"

A. "Well, that would be part of it. Right now she would like to work more than she's working."

Q. "You're saying she does have the desire to work more?"

A. "Yes. But, she also has the realization when she tries to do that, that it results in difficulty for her."

Q. "Now, is that because she also has a home life and children to blend in with the work responsibilities?"

A. "I don't know."

Q. "So, if we take away the responsibilities that have apparently concerned her about how her children are growing up, she might be able to work full time?"

A. "I don't know."

Q. "Okay. Have you recommended or prescribed any restrictions of any other kind on her in terms of activities?"

A. "No, not that I can remember."

Q. "She isn't restricted in her social activities in any way?"

A. "No."

Q. "She isn't restricted in her recreational activities in any way?"

A. "No."

Q. "She isn't restricted in where she can travel in any respect, is she?"

A. "No."

Q. "She isn't restricted in the type of people she should associate with or the type of environments in which she should find herself, or place herself, is she?"

A. "Not by me, no."

Q. "In other words, I guess I'll just combine it in one question, there are no lifestyle restrictions that you've placed on her, as your patient, other than in terms of how much she works?"

A. "Not entirely. I have advised her to find a living situation so she wouldn't have so much house to take care of and things of that nature, if that's what you're referring to."

Q. "Yes, it is what I'm referring to. Anything else along that line?"

A. "Not that I can think of right off hand."

Q. "Have you made any recommendation to her about dealing with her children?"

A. "We have discussions about her children many times. My advice being mostly that she should help them become as independent as they could so they would not be so dependent on her."

Q. "In other words, to accelerate the time in which they would be emancipated?"

A. "As much as realistic."

Q. "As much as reasonable?"

A. "Yes."

Q. "That's a recommendation that's good for any parent, isn't it?"

A. "For the most part, I would say yes."

Here is another example exploring lifestyle to negate the extent of disability caused by the alleged psychological condition:

Q. "She's been keeping house, doing washing and cooking and the normal things that a person who lives at home does?"

A. "She was not able to do all these particular nice things at the height of her depression. She is able to do that now."

Q. "She's been doing those things for a number of years?"

A. "I would say probably in the last two. As far as previously, I am not aware of."

Q. "She certainly hasn't ever been in a hospital for psychiatric treatment of any kind?"

A. "No."

Q. "And there hasn't been any nurse taking care of her?"

A. "No, sir."

Q. "She's been living at home on her own?"

A. "Yes, sir."

Q. "She has a child?"

A. "Yes, I believe so."

Q. "As far as you know, she is able to deal with the joys and problems of raising a child?"

A. "That I assume, sir."

Q. "You've certainly recorded no problems in that regard?"

A. "No, she's really not alluded to any."

Q. "Now, you see her about once a month?"

A. "Yes."

Q. "And this frequency of visits is not considered intensive therapy in your practice?"

A. "No, sir."

Q. "And you indicated that you expect to discharge her from your care soon?"

A. "I expect to get her off her anti-depressives, yes."

Q. "Do you expect not to have to see her anymore?"

A. "Yes, that's what I expect."

Q. "Now you indicated you know her husband through some Masonic group?"

A. "Yes."

Q. "And you understand your patient is a member of the Ladies' Oriental Shrine of North America?"

A. "I do."

Q. "Do you understand that that's a group which she's about to become the North American leader of?"

A. "I'm aware of that, yes."

Q. "She's discussed it with you?"

A. "Yes."

Q. "That's a group of about 16,000 women throughout the United States and Canada?"

A. "I don't know the exact number, but it's a large group."

Q. "Do you understand for the next year as Grand High Priestess of the group she will visit some 76 courts through the United States and Canada?"

A. "I'm aware of that, yes."

Q. "And each of those visits will be for two or three days?"

A. "Yes."

Q. "So she'll be away from home traveling on that significant honor for the better half of this year?"

A. "Yes, I'm aware of that."

Q. "You feel she can do it?"

A. "I feel she can give it a good try."

Q. "And to be this leader she's had to work her way up through various steps or chairs to be Grand High Priestess?"

A. "Yes."

Q. "And it's taken a number of years to achieve this top position?"

A. "Yes."

Q. "She's been able to do that, obviously, hasn't she?"

A. "She's succeeded in it, yes."

Q. "She's had to attend a good number of meetings and meet a fair number of people?"

A. "I would imagine, yes."

Q. "And she'd have to make a favorable impression on those people?"

A. "Yes."

Q. "And she'll be handling grievances and administrative affairs for the 16,000 members?"

A. "I suppose so."

Q. "And planning for all that travel and duties we discussed?"

A. "Yes."

Q. "And you understand she has a life outside her home and outside her Oriental Shrine activities, right?"

A. "I know she attends church regularly."

Q. "And is in a monthly bridge club?"

A. "She did make that known to me."

Few jurors would conclude that she is socially disabled in any way by her alleged psychological condition. The other way to mitigate damages is to demonstrate the patient's reluctance to undertake treatment or rehabilitation:

Q. "Now, doctor, you asked Mr. Thomas whether he had been to the Bureau of Vocational Rehabilitation, didn't you?"

A. "Yes."

Q. "He told you he hadn't participated in any rehabilitation, didn't he?"

A. "Yes."

Q. "In fact, doctor, you received an application from the Bureau of Vocational Rehabilitation to complete for Mr. Thomas, didn't you?"

A. "Yes."

Q. "You never completed that form?"

A. "No, sir."

Q. "And your usual course of business is to have your secretary call the referring attorney to find out if you should complete the form?"

A. "Yes."

Q. "Did you complete the form in this case?"

A. "No."

Q. "In fact, doctor, it was your impression that Mr. Thomas was not interested in rehabilitation, wasn't it?"

A. "It was my impression he was turned down for rehabilitation because he was too nervous. This was told to me by the patient. So whether he was interested in rehabilitation or not, I cannot answer that specifically."

Q. "Did he tell you who at the Bureau told him he was too nervous?"

A. "No."

Q. "Did you ask him?"

A. "I did not."

Q. "So you don't know if that was his decision that he was too nervous or if it was someone else's, do you?"

A. "All I know is what he told me."

Q. "Doctor, wasn't it your impression that Mr. Thomas was not interested in rehabilitation?"

A. "I believe I said that in my report that he was not interested at this time."

Mr. Minor: "Thank you doctor. I have no further questions."

Here is another "lack of treatment" approach that also raises the implication that there is no real need for treatment:

Q. "Now, doctor, referring back to the lawyer's letter, you were told Mr. Thomas has seen three other psychiatrists, correct?"

A. "Yes."

Q. "One was Dr. Gould?"

A. "Yes."

Q. "And he did not treat Mr. Thomas for any psychiatric condition, did he?"

A. "No."

Q. "One was Dr. Halas?"

A. "Yes."

Q. "And he did not treat him for any psychiatric condition, did he?"

A. "Not to my knowledge."

Q. "And Mr. Thomas never told you he had ever received any psychiatric treatment?"

A. "That's correct. He never told me he received psychiatric treatment."

CHAPTER 10

UNUSUAL CROSS-EXAMINATIONS

"Don't become a mere recorder of facts, but try to penetrate the mystery of their origin."

—Ivan Pavlov (1849–1936)

10.1 The Compromised Expert
10.2 How It Looks at Trial—Whistleblower Case
10.3 Cross-Examination of Dr. Binger in the Alger Hiss Trial

Approaches to cross-examining psychiatrists and psychologists remain the same even when the context changes. Three examples are presented in this chapter.

10.1 THE COMPROMISED EXPERT

In rare instances, evidence of an expert's partiality may present itself if discovery is conducted properly:

Q. "In this case you examined Lauren Johnson on behalf of attorneys Mr. Jurus and Mr. Hunter?"

A. "Yes."

Q. "Attorney Workman here today is also with Mr. Jurus?"

A. "Yes."

Q. "Now, I believe you said you examined between 100 and 200 patients for Mr. Jurus this year?"

A. "Yes."

Mr. Workman: "Objection."

Court: "Overruled."

A. "Yes, I would say so, yes. I haven't the exact numbers."

Q. "I understand. There have been a lot, doctor. You've been performing psychiatric examinations on behalf of Mr. Jurus for a period of five or six years; is that correct?"

A. "Yes."

Q. "And you also examine patients for other attorneys who represent plaintiffs in cases of this type; is this correct?"

A. "I would say that, yes."

Q. "You do not perform as many psychiatric examinations for any other attorney as you do for Mr. Jurus, do you?"

Mr. Workman: "Objection."

Court: "Overruled. You may answer."

A. "That's doubt—probably not, I would say."

Q. "In the last year, you've appeared live or by deposition on several occasions on behalf of the plaintiffs represented by Mr. Jurus; is that correct?"

A. "Yes, I would say that."

Q. "And in the last year you have never testified either live or by deposition on behalf of an employer or defense counsel; is that correct?"

A. "That is so, yes."

Q. "Doctor, I will hand you what has been marked as Exhibits 1 through 20 and ask you whether those are copies of twenty different psychiatric examination reports from you addressed to Mr. Jurus or his associate, Mr. Hunter, between January 1996 and May 2001?"

Discussion held off the record.

A. "Yes."

Q. "In each, the name of the patient has been blacked out?"

A. "Yes."

Q. "Doctor, each of those twenty exhibits is a true and accurate copy of the original letter you sent to Mr. Jurus; is that correct?"

A. "Yes."

Q. "In each of those twenty cases, Mr. Jurus or Mr. Hunter represented the claimant or plaintiff; is that true?"

Mr. Workman: "Objection."

Court: "Overruled, you may answer."

A. "Yes."

Q. "In every single case you were asked to determine whether Mr. Jurus' client suffered from a psychiatric disability which was related to a physical injury; is that correct?"

A. "That is so, yes."

Q. "And in twenty out of twenty cases represented by those letters, you found a direct and proximate causal relationship between some psychiatric disorder and the industrial injury; is that correct?"

A. "I think so, yes."

Q. "Now, doctor, I will also hand you what has been marked as Exhibits 1-A, 2-A, 7-A, 9-A, 13-A, and 15-A. Are those exhibits supplemental letters which you addressed to Mr. Jurus?"

A. "Yes, yes."

Q. "And each of those supplemental exhibits is a true and accurate copy of the original letters to Mr. Jurus; is that correct?"

A. "I believe so, yes."

Q. Doctor, I would ask you to turn to Exhibit 15 and its accompanying supplemental letter, Exhibit 15-A. Do you have those exhibits before you, doctor?"

A. "Yes, I have, yes."

Q. "Now, doctor, Exhibit 15 is a letter addressed to Mr. Jurus dated December 9, 2000; is that correct?"

Mr. Workman: "Objection. Relevance."

Court: "Overruled."

A. "Yes, yes."

Q. "And Exhibit 15 discusses your examination of a patient who sustained an injury at work in September 1978; is that correct?"

A. "That is so, yes."

Q. "In Exhibit 15, the injury at work preceded your examination in that case by 22 years; is that correct?"

A. "Yes, that is so, yes."

Q. "Now, doctor, on Page 2 of Exhibit 15 you state, quote, I doubt that the onset of this neurosis can be attributed as a direct and proximate consequence of the injury which he suffered at work on September, 1978, close quote. Is that your statement?"

A. "That is my statement, yes."

Q. "Doctor, one of your reservations was that 22 years had elapsed between the accident and your examination; is that correct?"

A. "I cannot—I had that reservation at that time, is that it?"

Q. "Yes, was it one of your reservations?"

A. "Yes. I cannot recall, you know, what reservations I did have at that time, you know, but I mean I did make that statement at that time."

Q. "Doctor, would you please turn to Exhibit 15-A?"

A. "Yes."

Q. "And confirm that Exhibit 15-A is dated April 29, 2001?"

A. "Yes."

Q. "Doctor, before you prepared Exhibit 15-A, you did not reexamine Mr. Jurus' client?"

A. "I didn't. No, I didn't."

Q. "Nevertheless, in Exhibit 15-A you reversed your former opinion to find a direct and proximate relationship between the injury and the psychiatric condition; is that correct?"

A. "I did do that, yes."

Q. "Now, doctor, I'm done with the exhibits."

10.2 How It Looks at Trial—Whistleblower Case

Here is a trial transcript in a case in which a whistleblower is suing his employer, a waste management company, for damages for an alleged retaliatory firing. The employee, a PhD chemist, claims that the harassment by the Company caused or contributed to his paranoid schizophrenia. In other words, the Company's retaliation drove him crazy. The Company maintained that they fired him for poor performance and for making false reports to the Environmental Protection Agency, that the Company did not harass him, and that he was delusional.

The employee's psychological injury claim was supported by a psychologist. Even though the factual presentation is unusual, the topic headings show that the areas of cross-examination remain basically the same:

Q. "Doctor, as you recall, I'm Alan Radnor. I took your deposition last month; is that correct?"

A. "Yes."

Q. "You have been fair with Mr. Delli Bovi, I hope you will be equally fair with me on my questions today."

A. "Uh-huh."

Q. "You have to answer for the record."

A. "Yes."

Qualifications

Q. "Now, doctor, isn't it true that the university only allows you a limited time for private practice to see patients like Paul Phan on a private basis; isn't that true?"

A. "I'm not sure what you mean by limited, I can spend a full day a week."

Q. "In fact, however, you don't spend a full day a week, you spend, I think you told me, way less than five percent of your time seeing private patients; is that correct?

A. "Yes."

Q. "And that many of the patients you do see in your private practice involve something called biofeedback; is that right?"

A. "Yes."

Q. "And that's people with headaches and high blood pressure, you teach them a technique to help them control their headaches and things; is that right?"

A. "Basically."

Q. "And you wouldn't treat Paul Phan with biofeedback; would you?"

A. "No, I wouldn't."

Q. "He has a much different problem, doesn't he?"

A. "Absolutely."

Q. "And your research interest and area is biofeedback, is it not? Many of the presentations—"

A. "It's one of them, psychophysiology, yes."

Q. "And doctor, Dr. Phan is psychotic; is that correct?"

A. "That's correct."

Q. "And most of the patients you see are not psychotic, is that correct?"

A. "I'm not sure I would say most of them. We see a lot of psychotics."

Q. "I'm just asking what you told me in the deposition. Most of the patients you see are not psychotic, they would be neurotic or other types of problems?"

A. "I believe you asked me in my private practice, not in my university work."

Q. "Right; is that correct?"

A. "In my private practice, yes."

Q. "And doctor, you have not recently seen a paranoid or delusional patient in your private practice; is that correct?"

A. "In my private practice?"

Q. "Right."

A. "No."

Q. "And doctor, in fact, you only have one or two paranoid schizophrenics in your private practice; is that correct, at any given time?"

A. "I believe I said that."

Not a Psychiatrist

Q. "And, doctor, in this particular case, it would be your opinion that Dr. Phan, and I think he probably is on some medication, he should be taking medication; is that correct?"

A. "Yes, I would think he should."

Q. "And if you were treating a patient needing medication such as Dr. Phan, you would have to either refer that patient to a psychiatrist, who is an M.D., or another M.D. and work with that person; is that correct?"

A. "That's correct."

Q. "And, doctor, you don't treat any in-patient hospitalized patients, do you, in the hospital?"

A. "Not now, no."

Q. "Okay, and your professional address for your private practice that's out of your home; is that correct?"

A. "That's correct."

Q. "And you are not a member of any hospital staff, are you?"

A. "No."

Not Member of Professional Society

Q. "As a psychologist, you can become certified in psychology by taking a national examination by the American Board of Professional Psychology and become a diplomat; is that right?"

A. "That's right."

Q. "And you have never taken that?"

A. "I saw no need to."

Q. "And you have never become certified by the American Board of Professional Psychology, have you?"

A. "No."

Relationship with Lawyers

Q. "Now, doctor, so that the jury understands your role in this case, Dr. Phan, I believe you told me, didn't come to you to seek treatment, he was sent there by his lawyers, the Murrays; is that correct?"

A. "That's correct."

Q. "And you received a call from Dennis Murray, his lawyer; is that correct?"

A. "That's right."

Q. "And you believe that, I don't think they brought this out, but you have reviewed other cases for the Murrays, have you not?"

A. "Yes."

Q. "And that number would be about four, as best you can remember?"

A. "I believe, yes."

Payment

Q. "Now, doctor, when I took your deposition, your current charges were around 13, $1,400, at that time, for this examination; is that correct?"

A. "For the—"

Q. "And testing?"

A. "For the examinations, testing and court preparation. Yes."

Standard Psychological Facts

Q. "Now, doctor, your diagnosis in this case is paranoid schizophrenia, and I won't get into the philosophical debate about delusional paranoia, but your diagnosis is paranoid schizophrenia; is that correct?"

A. "Yes, that was my original diagnosis."

Q. "And that's a disease that's recognized, that is recognized in all cultures of the world, is it not?"

A. "Pretty much, yes."

Q. "And it's a disease that occurs at all levels of society; is that correct?"

A. "Yes."

Q. "It can occur among even the very intelligent; is that correct?"

A. "Oh, yes."

Q. "And often does?"

A. "Yes."

. . .

Q. "Doctor, isn't it true that paranoid schizophrenia is the most common of psychotic diseases?"

A. "It's one of them, yes."

Q. "And that often, and this is important, often schizophrenics function in society for long periods of time; isn't that true?"

A. "Yes."

Using Textbook

Q. "And in fact, I think you're familiar with Kolb's book because I noticed you had some of those articles in your files and I would like to discuss some of those now. Are you familiar with Demming studies which indicate that for every hospitalized schizophrenic in New York there were probably three who live in the community. Are you familiar with those studies?"

A. "They are hypotheses about most mental disorders of that nature and that's also true of paranoid delusional disorder."

Q. "So, even though someone may have a paranoid delusional disorder, or even a delusional disorder, they can and do function in society and can and do appear normal at times; is that correct?"

A. "Yes, sir."

Q. "So, you would not find it unusual, in spite of your diagnosis in 1985, that you knew Dr. Phan, within two minutes, was very ill, that in 1986, 1988, and thereafter, people hired him; are you aware of that?"

A. "Yes, I know he was hired. I'm not certain that he lasted very long."

Q. "Right, and we'll get to that, doctor, but you wouldn't be surprised that people hired him?"

A. "No."

Q. "And, in fact, they did?"

A. "Sure."

Q. "Now, doctor, the disease you describe, paranoid schizophrenia has a slow or rapid onset, doesn't it?"

A. "Slow or rapid, that's true for an awful lot of disorders. It's not a distinguishing characteristic."

Q. "I'm sorry. Are you finished?"

A. "As I said, it's not a distinguishing characteristic of, really, many disorders, because lots can be slow and lots can be fast, unfortunately."

Q. "And, doctor, according to Kolb's book, the symptoms of paranoid schizophrenia appear as early as the adolescent years, 16, even a little later at 25; isn't that true?"

A. "Yes, I'm aware of that."

Q. "And are you aware that when Dr. Phan came to the United States, when he immigrated to the United States, how old he was?"

A. "I don't recall, I would have to do the arithmetic, but I would say—"

Q. "Would you accept he was about 32 in 1970?"

A. "I certainly would accept that."

Q. "And, doctor, would you agree that paranoids are most often married and employed when the disease occurs?"

A. "Many are."

Q. "And doctor, there's been some talk about family illness, I would like to talk about that because you did say there was, and I don't know your exact words, some familial elements of this disease?"

A. "There are in most psychotic disorders, certainly."

Q. "And certainly in this?"

A. "Certainly."

Q. "You're not denying that?"

A. "Oh, no."

Q. "And familial means one of two things, I'm not sure where you're coming from, but it means either there is a genetic substrate, there is some sort of genetic problem, correct?"

A. "Yes, usually."

Q. "Or the family relationships?"

A. "That's what you try to sort out, of course, in genetic studies and familial is a general term that can imply both things."

Q. "And both of those can be involved and are in paranoid schizophrenia in people like Dr. Phan; is that correct?"

A. "We don't know, probably."

Q. "Probably, I'll accept that, doctor."

A. "I don't know."

Q. "We don't know because, and we'll talk about the evidence you have and the history you got, okay, in a minute?"

A. "Sure."

. . .

Q. "And would you agree that evidence of family illness is often absent in a history?"

A. "Oh, yes."

Q. "That doesn't mean that it isn't there, does it?"

A. "We don't know."

Q. "Who do you rely on your history for? Go ahead. Who do you rely on your history for, doctor?"

A. "In this case, from the patient."

Q. "Dr. Phan?"

A. "That's right."

Q. "Now, doctor, it's true, is it not, that a normal course of this disease, a normal course of someone who has paranoid schizophrenia is, at first, their delusions are limited and focused on one area, and then they naturally expand into other areas, isn't that correct?"

A. "Yes."

Q. "And that they become changeable and illogical; is that correct?"

A. "Yes."

Q. "And that the patient's grip on reality is loosened; is that correct?"

A. "That's correct."

Q. "Now, for the paranoid, doctor, whether it be Dr. Phan or any of the other tens of thousands of these people, the most common delusion that they have is that of persecution, isn't it, that somebody's out to get them?"

A. "That's a very common delusion."

Q. "And that's the delusion that Paul Phan has, isn't it?"

A. "Yes."

Q. "Doctor, is it fair to say that ideas of persecution by people, by employers, by the FBI, by anything, are common characteristics of paranoids no matter where they work?"

A. "No matter where—"

Q. "They work?"

A. "Yes."

Q. "Now, doctor, finally, one of the characteristics of a paranoid or paranoid schizophrenia is grandiosity; is that correct?"

A. "It can be, it needn't be."

Q. "They think they are better than everybody else; is that correct?"

A. "If they have grandiosity."

Q. "Well, you have in your notes some grandiose ideas of—"

A. "Yeah, if one has that, that's, grandiose means that, yes."

Q. "Do you recall you have in your notes that Dr. Phan expressed that to you?"

A. "Oh, yes."

Q. "And what were those ideas? Did you—"

A. "Yeah, I think that this grandiosity came in, I believe, it was in my second interview with him in terms of talking about money. Money is a very common grandiose kind of thing, money means nothing, that kind of thing, spending money is a grandiose kind of thing one sees in a number of disorders."

Q. "Do you recall our discussion on that, doctor? He said money meant nothing to him, but you had a different opinion, didn't you?"

A. "I don't recall what you are referring to, sir."

Q. "Okay, doctor, what's projection?"

A. "Projection is putting your needs out on someone else."

Q. "And do you recall our discussion regarding his ideas of money and him saying it doesn't mean much to him; what was your feeling about whether money really meant something to him?"

A. "It was hard to tell. It was like, who knows. He felt that this was a way, I think, to be grandiose. I think it made him feel good and important."

Q. "That he was spending a lot of money?"

A. "That he had money, I don't know if he has money and that he could spend all sorts of money, and I don't know that he spent money. I think that's the kind of thing that grandiosity is. If one goes out and spends lots of money that they don't have. That's grandiose."

Q. "Did you record any other ideas of grandiosity of Dr. Phan in your notes?"

A. "I don't recall off hand."

Expert's Report

Q. "Doctor, you listed, and you can refer to your records if you wish to during this examination."

A. "Okay."

Q. "You listed on a blank sheet, the characteristics of schizophrenia."

A. "Uh-huh."

Q. "Okay, and you listed four of these and this was in connection with your examination of Dr. Phan; is that correct?"

A. "Yeah, I'm not sure why that was in there, but yes."

Q. "And one was evidence of a thinking disorder?"

A. "Yes, sir."

Q. "And the other one was impaired perceptual accuracy or reality testing?"

A. "Yes."

Q. "And what you meant by that is the way he perceives things is not correct, he misperceives or misinterprets events; is that correct?"

A. "That's correct."

Q. "And he has evidence of that, right?"

A. "Absolutely."

Q. "And you saw evidence of that, did you not?"

A. "Yes."

Q. "And he's not reliable about what's going on there; is that correct?"

A. "He is not."

Q. "And, doctor, you further said he had poor emotional control; is that correct?"

A. "That's correct."

Q. "And finally, he had a limited or ineffective interpersonal life; is that correct?"

A. "That's correct."

Q. "And by that you mean he would not get along with people and not be able to trust people on any level; is that correct?"

A. "At this point in time, I think that's correct."

Other Causes

Q. Now, Doctor, let's talk about some of the factors and causes or contributions to the development of paranoid schizophrenia; is that fair?"

A. "That's fair."

Q. "Now, you would agree that the causes of this problem, be it paranoid schizophrenia or delusional disorder are complex, right?"

A. "Yes."

Q. "And there are multiple, I mean, there are many causes; is that correct?"

A. "More than one."

Q. "Is there a sole cause for this condition?"

A. "There is no evidence, in my opinion, that there is a sole cause."

Q. "And in every book that you teach, for instance, Sarason's book; are you familiar with that?"

A. "Sure."

Q. "Does it discuss the genetic causes and contributions of genetics and family life to this problem?"

A. "Yes."

Q. "Do they not?"

A. "Certainly."

Q. "Doctor, would you agree that early maternal history and development are also important in development of paranoid schizophrenia?"

A. "Yes."

Q. "And can be a contributing cause to the problem?"

A. "Yes."

Q. "And could be a contributing cause in Paul Phan's case?"

A. "It could be, I don't know."

Q. "And, we'll get to your history in a minute, doctor. And later family relationships can also be important, can they not, doctor?"

A. "Yes."

Q. "And they can be contributing causes in these types of problems, be it paranoid schizophrenia or delusional disorders?"

A. "Uh-huh."

Q. "Is that correct?"

A. "Yes."

Q. "And you believe that other stressors can contribute to this problem; is this correct?"

A. "Yes."

Q. "And so that the jury is clear, you have testified that there are always other factors that contribute to this disease; is that correct?"

A. "I don't think I said there are always other factors, I think there can be other factors in any given point in time."

Q. "Doctor, do you remember I took your deposition on July 8, last month of this year; do you recall that?"

A. "Yes, I do."

The Court: Do you want to give a page?

Mr. Radnor: Page 52.

Q. "Doctor, I think you have testified you didn't believe you said to me, always. Let me read you this question on page 52 of your deposition. Question: 'And that is when you say contribution, is it a factor, there are other factors that also contributed; is that fair?' And your answer was, 'Yes, there are always other factors.' Do you recall that question and that answer?"

A. "I think so, yes."

Q. "Now, doctor, there is no dispute that, at least in part, Waste Management is a focus of Dr. Phan's delusions; is that correct?"

A. "Yes."

Q. "And when we say focus, we mean that the delusional or paranoid person picks an event to misperceive, misconstrue and then feels he is persecuted by that particular event; is that correct?"

A. "That's correct."

Q. "And with these types of people, that can happen when they are sitting in front of the television; is that correct, and something triggers their mind that something is wrong; is that correct?"

A. "I suppose it's possible."

Q. "It can happen in relation to somebody's family, that a spouse is persecuting them?"

A. "I see what you mean, yes."

Q. "It can happen in relation to where they work other than Waste Management; is that correct?"

A. "I'm sure."

Q. "Okay now, there is no denying that Dr. Phan's—part of his focus in this case is Waste Management, do you agree with that?"

A. "Oh, yes."

Conflicting, Incomplete History

Q. "Now, let's get to the history that you obtained in this case, doctor. In determining what disease somebody has and what contributes, history is very important, is it not?"

A. "Yes."

Q. "An accurate and complete history is important in that regard, in determining—"

A. "Yes."

Q. "—the cause and contributions of disease; is that correct?"

A. "Yes."

Q. "And an inaccurate or incomplete history would lead to a faulty conclusion or opinion about a patient; isn't that true?"

A. "It's possible."

Q. "You teach that to your students, don't you?"

A. "Uh-huh, yes."

Q. "Now, there's two parts to taking a history, are there not; one is you must ask the right questions; is that correct?"

A. "Yes."

Q. "And the second is you must rely on what the patient tells you?"

A. "Yes, if that's all you have available to you."

Q. "Sure."

A. "Certainly."

Q. "I'm not debating that."

A. "Oh, okay, I didn't understand what you were debating."

Q. "But there is an art to bringing out what the history of a patient is, right?"

A. "I think so."

Q. "And some patients are resistant to giving you their full history; is that correct?"

A. "Some patients are."

Q. "And, doctor, in getting that history, is a discussion of childhood experiences important?"

A. "Yes."

Q. "Discussion of family relationships is important?"

A. "Yes."

Q. "Discussion of marriage is important?"

A. "Yes."

Q. "Now, doctor, you met with this gentleman three times?"

A. "Yes."

Q. "How many pages of handwritten notes do you have on this gentleman?"

A. "Oh, I don't know about five, something like that."

Q. "Four."

A. "Four? Okay."

Q. "The first visit you had with him you took about three pages of notes, right?"

A. "Yes."

Q. "And the second visit, and as I understand your normal routine, you take notes and you do a typed summary which are also in your records; is that correct?"

A. "Yes."

Q. "And you usually take notes and then type up a summary; is that right?"

A. "Yes."

Q. "Now, the second time you saw him, you didn't take any notes, did you?"

A. "I don't know about that, I'm uncertain."

Q. "You didn't give me any notes you took during that second visit?"

A. "I don't have any notes from that time and I'm not certain what that is."

Q. "And, it's of some concern because that's unusual for you, isn't it?"

A. "Not to have them? Yes."

Q. "Do you recall Paul Phan asked you not to take notes?"

A. "I'm not certain. I think he may have or he may have gotten upset when I began taking notes."

Q. "So you stopped?"

A. (Nod indicating yes.) "Yes, I believe, but I simply can't recall. I have tried to remember that and I just can't."

Q. "And, in your three visits with him including your typewritten summaries, you have about six pages of notes; is that correct, including the handwritten notes and typewritten summaries?"

A. "Yes."

Q. "Now, doctor, you can refer to your notes for the following questions. Did you record in your notes anywhere that Dr. Phan had dead bodies on his doorstep when he was growing up?"

A. "No."

Q. "He didn't tell you that?"

A. "No."

Q. "Did you record anywhere that he applied to medical school and didn't get in?"

A. "No."

Q. "Did you record anywhere that he thought people in the Maryland laboratory where he worked before Waste Management cheated him and that they were not honest?"

A. "No, I did not."

Q. "Did you record that students threatened to kill him or at least he believed that if he didn't get good—give them good grades—"

A. "Did I record that? No, I did not."

Q. "Did you record that he claimed a priest in Maryland cheated him in connection with buying a car?"

A. "No, sir."

Q. "In terms of his Maryland experience, if I read your notes correctly, all you recorded was that he was a teaching assistant and had a Master's in food technology at the University of Maryland; is that correct?"

A. "I'm not sure, I would have to look, but if that's all that's in there about Maryland, I knew he told me about Maryland and working for a company there, and that sort of thing. I don't write everything down."

Q. "Okay. Doctor, you did record that first visit, though, a piece of information of experiences before Waste Management, did you not?"

A. "Yes, I did."

Q. "And that was in connection with his work at Kal-Kan in Columbus; is that correct?"

A. "Yes."

Q. "And what you recorded there, doctor, if I can put this on the board, was that you had a long discussion about how businesses are not honest, I'm using your exact words, he was always honest, and you put there, 'this apparently before job at Waste Management'; is that correct, doctor?"

A. "Yes, I see that."

Q. "And doctor, do you recall, did you record anything else about that long discussion you had?"

A. "No, because it involved his really long dissertating that all businesses are dishonest."

Q. "And this is 1985?"

A. "This is 1985, yes."

Q. "And you made the entry thinking that there were some psychological problems with this man before Waste Management; isn't that true?"

A. "I was trying to find out, sir."

Q. "Well, you would not deny that, would you, doctor?"

A. "Deny what?"

Q. "That there were some psychological problems with this man?"

A. "I was trying to find out, that's what I was attempting to find out."

Q. "And you wouldn't be doing your job if you weren't doing that; is that correct?"

A. "I think so."

Q. "And doctor, isn't it true that you made that entry thinking that there was some problem before waste Management, isn't that fair?

A. "Uh-huh."

Q. "And I asked you the following questions, page 72, line 22."

Q. (Reading) "Question: 'In these complaints here, you made that entry perhaps thinking there was some problem before Waste Management; is that right fair?' And your answer was, 'Certainly.' Is that correct?"

A. "Yes, I assume."

Q. "Would you like to look at that?"

The Court: Page again, Mr. Radnor, was 72?

Mr. Radnor: Seventy-three, Your Honor.

Q. "Now doctor, in your notes did you record what those problems were at Kal-Kan?"

A. "I don't recall. I don't see it. I remember what we are talking about."

Q. "Do you remember what those problems were?"

A. "I remember one of the things he said, yes."

Q. "What was that?"

A. "Something about watering down food, dog food."

Q. "What about violation of FDA standards, was he complaining to you about that?"

A. "No, I don't know, I don't recall that, it was watering down the dog food, so the people weren't getting enough, so the business wasn't honest."

Q. "What about improper analysis, did you get that history?"

A. "He didn't say anything about that."

Q. "What about he claimed that they asked him to cheat, did you get that history?"

A. "To cheat? I don't recall that, no. I recall he suspected that business of watering down the food and this kind of thing and I don't, that's what that reference is."

Q. "Okay now, doctor, did you get any history about his business, PLP Foods, and the problems he had with that, or claimed he had?"

A. "I heard about his food company, yes."

Q. "And what else did you record?"

A. "What else did I—"

Q. "Record in your notes?"

A. "What else did I record? I'm sorry."

Q. "Did you record any problems he had with his business?"

A. "Apparently, the business, just he said he wasn't making enough money and his wife wanted him to get another job, so he stopped the business. That's what he told me and that was all that he told me."

Q. "And, doctor, did you record where he worked, and I think you did record where he worked after he worked at Waste Management; is that correct?"

A. "I'm not sure he told me precisely, that was not clear, and he was very hard to get some of that kind of information out of. He had a job in California, I understand."

Q. "I was talking about your history, generally, doctor."

A. "Which we were talking about, yes, I'm sorry, I thought you were talking about the first time I saw him. Last year he talked to me and I do have it recorded that he had trouble in jobs that he had since I had seen him, and I think there were these two jobs and we talked about those."

Q. "What did you record in that respect?"

A. "I think I said trouble at jobs."

Q. "That's all?"

A. "I would have to look. Trouble at Punta Gorda and try to prove I am wrong which was part of that—basically, it was the same sort of thing that he's, that he talked about earlier in that he felt that people were doing things wrong, and for some reason, he didn't keep those jobs. I think it's pretty clear why he didn't keep those jobs, because of his illness."

Q. "Doctor, in connection with the first interview that you had with him, was it fair to say that he reported two concerns to you in that first interview; one being with Waste Management and the Kal-Kan employers, and the other being his divorce situation; is that correct?"

A. "Yes, he did talk about his divorce, all connected to his problems, everything was related to his problems."

Psychological Testing

Q. "Okay, doctor, you did an MMPI; is that correct?"

A. "That's correct."

Q. "And you interpreted that as showing a paranoid schizophrenic; is that correct?"

A. "That's correct."

Q. "The test itself doesn't tell you anything about what caused the problem, does it?"

A. "No."

Q. "And that some results of the profile which you alluded to, on direct, the MMPI can be interpreted as showing longstanding problems; isn't that correct?"

A. "Longstanding problems?"

Q. "Yes."

A. "Well, remember, I saw him in 1985 and I don't know when that began."

Q. "Okay."

A. "So, I don't know what you mean by longstanding. A year?"

Q. "No, this was your testimony, doctor."

A. "I know."

Q. "It wasn't my testimony. Do you recall telling me that, in fact, an elevation of scale eight showed very longstanding problems or difficulties, do you recall that testimony?"

A. "No."

Q. "Page 82 of your deposition."

The Court: "You have it there, doctor?"

The Witness: "Yes."

Q. "I said, 'What clues did you have in terms of the graph as to significant longstanding problems with Dr. Phan in terms of his personality?' Your answer was: 'Longstanding problems, answer, line 11, certainly the elevations on eight, which was a profiles problematical and often indicative of very longstanding problems'."

A. "Yup."

Q. "Is that correct?

A. "Yes."

Q. "Now, Doctor, the personality characteristics that were discussed in that question, many of those personality characteristics are formed as a teenager or before; is that correct?"

A. "They can be."

Q. "Doctor, you felt that he was very socially introverted, or don't you recall telling me that?"

A. "I don't recall a discussion of that."

Q. "Turn to page 83."

A. "What are we talking about? Are we talking about the MMPI or—"

Q. "Look on page 83, doctor."

A. "Page 83."

Q. "Right, line 18."

A. "Uh-huh."

Q. "Your answer was socially introverted, you have a zero, and my question was, yeah, and your answer was, he was quite socially introverted?"

A. "Uh-huh."

Q. "Is that correct?"

A. "That's what it says."

Q. "And social introversion or extroversion—"

A. "No, you're missing—social introversion is the scale which is scale 0."

Q. "Right."

A. “That doesn’t mean it’s a score 0.”

Q. “No, I understand that.”

A. “That isn’t what you said.”

Q. “Well, did you—that’s not what I’m concerned about, doctor. You said he was quite socially introverted?”

A. “I think, overall, he is introverted or has been introverted, right.”

Q. “And that’s a personality characteristic that’s formed in childhood, is it not?”

A. “Somewhat early, sure, and we talked about that.”

Q. “And that would be before Waste Management; is that correct?”

A. “Yes.”

Q. “Doctor, when somebody is introverted, can you tell us what that means?”

A. “Introverted in the more technical sense means turned in, when a person is not terribly sociable, not a person we would call an outgoing, friendly kind of person. Introverted would be someone who perhaps is more shy, retiring, careful in their relationships with others. Does that help?”

Q. “And such a person may have problems with forming interpersonal relationships; is that correct?”

A. “Not necessarily. Well, you know, introverted people can have satisfying personal relationships, I mean, it’s one of these dimension kinds of things.”

Q. "Depending on the degree?"

A. "And depending on how introverted a person is. One can also be introverted and have one or two very close friends, but not be an outgoing kind of person. So, I don't think that it implies necessarily that they are not going to be able to form relationships. I think that's something we need to clarify there."

Q. "Your evaluation was that he was very socially introverted?"

A. "I think he is an introverted fellow."

Q. "And, doctor, in connection with your Rorschach, which was the inkblot test, that also will not tell you the cause of the problem; is that correct?"

A. "No, it won't tell you the cause."

Q. "But the Rorschach does give you basic insight into a person's personality from a very young age, isn't that true?"

A. "Well, it gives us some indication, at least, of how they are looking at the world, and how they are looking at it now. I'm not as sure about young age. I think that, you know, we had a discussion, I believe, about the reliability and validity of that also. But if you are looking at personality structure, we talked about that as being young age."

Q. "Age six, a very young age; is that correct?"

A. "That's young, that's young."

Q. "Do you recall that discussion?"

A. "We had a discussion of that."

Q. "And his Rorschach showed a very disturbed, abnormal personality; did it not?"

A. "The way he was functioning then, absolutely."

Q. "Now, doctor, I would like to talk about how he feels about Waste Management. First of all, you believe that he is, and we have talked about this, his reality testing is poor and that means his perception of what reality is is poor; is that correct?"

A. "Right."

Q. "Is that correct?"

A. "Yes."

Q. "And you know he has delusional or untrue ideas from your examination, the MMPI and the Rorschach, isn't that correct?"

A. "Yes."

Q. "But you do not know how long he has had these ideas, do you, doctor?"

A. "No."

Q. "And by definition, delusions are untrue. Somebody has these ideas, they are not—"

A. "That's how they are defined, they are false beliefs."

Q. "Right. And he has delusions about Waste Management that you admit, do you not?"

A. "Well, I hope they are delusions."

Q. "Okay, you believe they are delusions?"

A. "Yeah, I believe they are, I don't believe that the company is trying to kill him."

Q. "Sure. And you don't believe that the company burned down his house?"

A. "I would find, you know, all of that—that's the problem, all of these things are possible, but I don't think it's very probable."

Q. "Or planting bombs in his car?"

A. "No, all of it's possible. Probable, well, I don't think it's very probable, but I guess that's why I call them delusions, sure."

Q. "Right. And that's part of your diagnosis in this case?"

A. "Sure."

Q. "And planting bombs in cars is a classic delusion, is it not?"

A. "It's been around a while."

Q. "You have heard it before from other patients?"

A. "Sure."

Q. "Those who haven't worked at Waste Management, right?"

A. "Sure."

Q. "And you do not believe that Waste Management or anyone is following him around, do you?"

A. "I don't think so."

Q. "Or that they would undertake to follow him around forever?"

A. "I certainly don't think that's probable."

Q. "Now, doctor, going to your second meeting with Dr. Phan in May 1985, you can refer to your summary on that, I guess you don't have any handwritten notes?"

A. "Right."

Q. "You can refer to your summary. It is true, is it not, that you recorded in that summary that his major concerns during this interview centered on his recent involvement in a divorce action and the lack of contact with his children; is that correct?"

A. "Yes."

Q. "And that was—"

A. "I'm trying to find that."

Q. "—May 1985?"

A. "May 1985, yes, sir."

Q. "And, at that point, he had advised that he had three lawyers for his divorce; is that correct?"

A. "Yeah, and he couldn't trust any of them."

Q. "Everyone was lying to him; is that correct?"

A. "Yes."

Q. "And he wanted to kill them all; is that correct?"

A. "That's what he said."

Q. "And he gave money to a taxi driver and he kept the money; is that correct?"

A. "That was a—yes, there was a long, confused story. I don't know if you want to hear it or not."

Q. "Well, there were other stories like that. And none of that was in reference to Waste Management, his lawyers or any of that, was it?"

A. "Not those lawyers, no."

Q. "Doctor, did you review with him the problems that his wife was having with him at this time?"

A. "His wife was divorcing him and that had started sometime before that, and as I understand, this was the divorce action. Well, the story was very confused, I'm not sure what I understand."

Q. "Is divorce known as a stressful or stressor, stressful situation?"

A. "It certainly can be."

Q. "Were you aware that his wife got a restraining order to prevent him from harassing her or molesting her or her children?"

A. "I don't believe I was aware of that, but it doesn't surprise me."

Q. "Were you aware that Dr. Phan was flattening her tires and taking the distributor cap off of her car?"

A. "No, but it doesn't surprise me."

Q. "Do you report that he called the police on his wife because she was driving a car that they owned?"

A. "No."

Q. "Do you know how long they lived together in their ten years of marriage?"

A. "No."

Q. "You didn't get that?"

A. "The impression that I got was that it kind of went back and forth. I'm really not certain."

Q. "You didn't get any history of that?"

A. "I don't have anything that's, you know, strikes me as I can say. It sounded like things got stormy, but I'm not certain exactly when."

Q. "Who did he come to that interview with?"

A. "I don't know, someone."

Q. "Who? Well, you recorded something."

A. "Yeah, I don't know. He wouldn't tell me who it was. She was there. Do you want me to describe, I can describe who was there. He came with a female who he didn't introduce me to, who, as soon as she saw me, turned around and left. And I asked him who that was and he would not tell me. I don't know who it was, I don't know if it was his wife, I don't know if it was somebody who drove him, I don't know."

Q. "And doctor, at this point, you felt that his delusions were expanding; is that correct?"

A. "Oh, yes, they were expanding."

Q. "And you felt that the focus in the first interview was on his former employers, and in the, now, it had shifted to the most significant others in his environment?"

A. "It shifted, it included a lot of other people and not exclusively, it didn't leave the company, however."

Q. "Well, what you recorded—"

A. "Well, I recorded that because he—I also said, I believe, in that interview, he didn't trust Attorney Murray anymore because Mr. Murray was working for the company."

Q. "That was his other delusion?"

A. "Yeah, but I just see it hadn't shifted, and I told him he had to trust Mr. Murray and worked very strong on that, but he thought Mr. Murray was working for Waste Management."

Q. "Well, doctor, you recorded, did you not, that his, on the second page of that summary?"

A. "Right."

Q. "His focus was on his former employers in the first interview, it has now shifted—"

A. "Right."

Q. "—to the most significant others in his environment?"

A. "Right, the others, absolutely, yes."

Q. "That would be his wife, his lawyer, his divorce lawyers, all of these people; is that right?"

A. "Right."

Q. "And that's the normal course of this disease; is it not, or can be a normal course?"

A. "Yes, that's what concerned me."

Q. "And doctor, in the 1990 visit, there is an interesting entry entitled note that you made, and I don't believe you have a summary for 1990, just your handwritten notes; is that correct?"

A. "Right, that's correct."

Q. "I think you made a note: 'Enemies from the past'?"

A. "That's what I went after, yeah, that was one of the things where I was going and wrote down and kept trying to go after it to find out, you know, how all this thing, how long this thing has been around and—"

Q. "You couldn't get—"

The Court: "Let him finish. Are you finished, Doctor?"

A. "I don't think I was finished."

Q. "Sorry."

A. "I was concerned and I wanted to get at that kind of thing, and as he was expanding, I wanted to know if he was also now going to start talking about other, you know, expanded it to people in the past, etc. That information was not forthcoming. He did not talk about enemies from the past. I kept trying to get at that sort of thing, again, trying to do my job to get a sense of when this thing, this process started with this man, and trying to get a handle on it and that's all I was trying to do and that's what that note means. And I went after it and after it, I think that, you know, I pushed and pushed to try to get at those kinds of things from different ways, being sympathetic, talking about, you know, people misunderstanding him, all of that kind of thing that I wanted to do to draw this out to see if there were things back there. I couldn't find them."

Q. "You couldn't get them out of him?"

A. "I couldn't find them."

Q. "Okay, now, doctor—"

A. "As far as I'm concerned, at that point, they weren't there."

Q. "Okay now, doctor, you formed opinions in this case based on interviewing Dr. Phan and reading deposition testimony; is that correct?"

A. "Yes."

Q. "Did you ever review the medical records in this case?"

A. "No, I have not been given any medical records."

Q. "You have not reviewed any testimony of his fellow employees in this case?"

A. "No."

Q. "And you do not know how he was psychologically before 1981, do you; before 1985?"

A. "Before 1985, that's right."

Q. "You don't know; isn't that correct?"

A. "I don't know."

Alternate Hypothetical

Q. "And, doctor, assume that he was in some state, and you talked about a continuum, but in some state of paranoid schizophrenia or delusional disorder from 1979 to 1981 when he worked at Waste Management, okay?"

A. "All right."

Q. "Would it be fair to say, based on what you know of his problems, that that would affect his work performance?"

A. "If he were having the disorder at that time?"

Q. "Yes."

A. "Yes."

Q. "And it would affect his ability to get along with others, would it not, doctor?"

A. "Yes."

Q. "And it would cause problems at work, would it not, doctor?"

A. "I would think so."

Q. "And, if he was in a position of deciding what waste should be accepted and rejected, and he was delusional or a paranoid schizophrenic, that would be stressful for him, would it not?"

A. "I'm sorry."

Q. "If he was in the position of accepting or rejecting waste for that business, and he was a paranoid schizophrenic or delusional, that would be stressful, would it not, could be?"

A. "Yeah, I don't know, I'm, I really don't know how to answer that, whether or not it would be stressful for him to make a decision based on whatever chemical stuff that he based his decisions on, I don't know that would be stressful."

Q. "Doctor, these issues of affecting his work performance, ability to get along with others, causing problems at work, not feeling people were honest, if he was delusional before 1979, it would also cause problems where he worked before 1979, those same problems; is that correct?"

A. "I would expect so."

Q. "Okay, and doctor, you indicated that, in your opinion, the work at Waste Management was a contributing factor, I believe, when I took your deposition; isn't that true?"

A. "Uh-huh, yes."

Q. "And that's still your opinion today, is it not?"

A. "Yes."

Q. "And when you testified that it was a cause, you meant that in, at least your opinion, in the sense of a contributing factor?"

A. "I think they are the same things."

Q. "Okay, in your mind, fine. Now, doctor, that assumes, does it not, that there are other contributing factors?"

A. "Yes."

Q. "And you believe that in Paul Phan's case, necessarily based upon your testimony; is that correct, and your education and background?"

A. "Yes, I don't know what they all are."

Q. "You were not able to determine what they all are?"

A. "No."

Q. "And, in terms of what Waste Management did to this man, could you review your notes and tell us exactly what, in your notes, you found was contributory to his—or you believe based on the history I gave you, was contributory to these problems?"

A. "Well, I think you find most of it in when he began they helped him buy a house, they thought he was fine, he begins, he reported he began to find things wrong, he said he was made head chemist within a short period of time and it goes on like that, and then his becoming worried about what they were doing there and his feeling that it would be his fault."

Q. "What did he say exactly in that?"

A. "It 'will be my neck'."

Q. "Quote, my neck, unquote."

A. "And then he had a lot of how many and was questioning many one-time-only shipments are there going to be, that kind of thing was very concerned of him and the fine by the EPA that he reported, they began to get upset with him, they wanted him to stop what he was doing, that he was doing things that would harm the company. They sent him to Chicago to talk with others in the company. They told him to stop digging into the problems, something about an explosion and then being terminated in 4/81. That, basically, is the history that I have written in my notes, that was the kind of thing that he told me."

Q. "And you don't have any more detail than that; is that correct?"

A. "Not in my notes, no."

Q. "And Doctor, do you know how much of that history is accurate?"

A. "Only from, you know, reading his deposition that was his history and—that's all I can say."

Q. "And that's what your testimony is based on, right?"

A. "That's what it's been based on, sir."

Q. "Doctor, in a disease like paranoid schizophrenia, and I have a few more questions here, a disease like paranoid schizophrenia, your opinion is that other factors contribute and, in fact, you testified that they always contribute, we have gone over that?"

A. "Yes, sir."

Q. "Now, the fact that he was fired at Waste Management, fired at MBC, fired at Punta Gorda assumes those facts, those could all contribute to his problem; is that correct?"

A. "He had a problem by the time those other ones occurred."

Q. "May have had a problem at Waste Management, correct?"

A. "Correct."

Q. "And—"

A. "I know he had, let's get this straight, I know he had the problem on those other, by the time those other ones occurred because I had already seen him."

Q. "Right, and you don't have much—"

A. "And I already had that problem diagnosed, and it doesn't surprise me one bit."

Q. "And family history contributed, in your view, probably contributed?"

A. "We don't know."

Q. "Genetics contributed?"

A. "I don't know."

Q. "How about adjustment difficulties, can those contribute?"

A. "Stressors and adjustment difficulties can contribute, yes."

Q. "Now, stressors, for our purposes, can we just say stresses, everyday stresses?"

A. "Stresses."

Q. "And you have those in employment wherever you work, Kal-Kan, Waste Management, MBC, Punta Gorda, right?"

A. "Well, some people do, some people don't, you know."

Q. "Depends on your reaction to that; is that correct?"

A. "Depends on what happens, it's not just the reaction, it also depends on the nature of the job. Some jobs aren't very stressful, some jobs are, you know, I think we all run into that sort of thing."

Q. "Doctor, here he only gave you much information on Kal-Kan and Waste Management; is that correct?"

A. "That's correct except for those post-1985 ones."

Q. "And marital relationships—"

A. "And 1990 ones."

Q. "Yeah. So that I can get to this, marital relationships can be stressful, right?"

A. "Yes."

Q. "Or they can be pleasant?"

A. "Or they can be great."

Q. "And, if Dr. Phan felt he was forced into his first marriage and believed that his first child was not his, could that be a stressor that contributes to this problem?"

A. "To this problem? I don't know but it could be a stressor."

Q. "Sure. And if his family rejected his first wife, could that also be a stressor?"

A. "Are we talking about the same wife?"

Q. "The first wife, yes."

A. "Right, that could be a stress for a person."

Q. "Right."

A. "Sure."

Q. "Doctor, not seeing his children could be stressful and contributory to a psychological condition such as paranoid schizophrenia?"

A. "For some people, certainly."

Q. "And being involved, as we see, in a divorce lawsuit, can be stressful to certain individuals with paranoid schizophrenia?"

A. "Yes."

Q. "And doctor, Dr. Phan expressed to you that he wanted to punish Waste Management, his wife, the world; is that correct?"

A. "Eventually, yeah, he was at the point where he wanted to punish everything."

Q. "Now, doctor, he gave you a brochure to show you how successful his family was; is that correct?"

A. "That's correct."

Q. "If someone perceives they are not as successful as their family, is it fair to say that that can contribute to psychological conditions?"

A. "Again, if that occurs and if there is a stress, it could contribute."

Q. "Now, Doctor—"

A. "There are all sorts of stressors that exist in the world, if that's what we are talking about."

Q. "Right, and it's our reaction to them that determines a lot about us, isn't it?"

A. "Uh-huh, and whether or not we even perceive them."

Q. "Now doctor, you wrote that from January to May you saw him in January and May of 1985?"

A. "Uh-huh."

Q. "He got worse?"

A. "In my opinion, yes."

Q. "And you don't have any opinion as to the cause, right?"

A. "I don't know why he got worse. We talked about that, deterioration of the disorder that is the progressive down-hill nature of the disorder, that kind of thing, I think, we did talk about that, didn't we?"

Q. "And stressors can affect you also?"

A. "Sure."

Q. "And during that time, he was going through his divorce; is that correct?"

A. "That's what he told me."

Q. "And he was not in the employ of Waste Management at that time; is that correct?"

A. "Oh, no, not as far as I'm aware."

Q. "And, in 1990, when you saw him he was not as distraught or emotionally upset; is that correct?"

A. "He didn't seem to be, although, everything was still there. I thought he was calmer."

Q. "Okay."

A. "But, it was all still there, unfortunately, it was not better."

Q. "I'm sorry?"

A. "It was not better; part of that may have been that he was more used to me by then."

Q. "Are you done?"

A. "Yes."

Q. "Doctor, I would like to ask you a question and this is important. Is it fair to say that you cannot say, to a reasonable degree of psychological certainty, or make a judgment as to the amount of contribution employment at Waste Management contributed or aggravated his paranoid schizophrenic problems; isn't that true?"

A. "I cannot make that statement. I think that's true."

Q. "Doctor, assume the MMPI and the Rorschach you took of Dr. Phan, the symptoms you recorded and behaviors you recorded of him except for his complaints about Waste Management, further assume that he was fired from his job in Florida, that he was divorced, could not see his children for a time; is it fair to say that it's your opinion to a reasonable degree of psychological certainty, if Dr. Phan presented the same behaviors, you would diagnose him in the same way?"

A. "May I make sure I understand the question?"

The Court: Absolutely.

A. "The question is that if, we are assuming that he was never employed at Waste Management, but I saw him in 1985 without having been employed at Waste Management, on the behaviors that I saw in 1985 and 1990, I would still call him paranoid schizophrenic?"

Q. "Including your MMPI and Rorschach."

A. "Yes, I would still call him a paranoid schizophrenic."

Secondary Gain

Q. "Good, thank you. Doctor, what is secondary gain?"

A. "Secondary gain is a type of, I want to say satisfaction, I need a word different than gain, or a type of gratification, and again it's hard to get away from gain, gets circular in defining it, but that a person might derive from a symptom. For example, if my back hurts, I might derive some secondary gain in all sorts of nice, tender, loving care from my wife. In addition to getting some kind of gain for my symptoms, eliciting some sort of a gain."

Q. "Psychological diseases, be they paranoid schizophrenia or mild neurosis sometimes have a component of secondary gain?"

A. "Sometimes, it's more common with neuroses, it is much more common in that area."

Q. "And in the litigation context, what is secondary gain for being ill?"

A. "In the litigation context, it's usually money."

Never Treated

Q. "And doctor, you didn't give any formal treatment to Dr. Phan in spite of the fact you felt he should be hospitalized; is that correct?"

A. "That's correct."

Mitigating Damages

Q. "But you told him to get on with his life, did you not?"

A. "I certainly did."

Q. "And to take personal responsibility for his actions?"

A. "I think so, something like that. I wanted him to try to leave this behind him, try to put his life back together. But, you know, with the severity of this disorder, you can't call that treatment. They were suggestions for helping this man. This is a pitiful man, at this point."

Q. "And doctor, you felt he should trust somebody; is that correct?"

A. "I would hope so."

Q. "And you told him that?"

A. "Yes."

Q. "And that he needed to disregard his fears?"

A. "Try to."

Q. "And you felt these were reasonable suggestions, right?"

A. (Nod indicating yes.)

Q. "For him?"

A. "Uh-huh."

Q. "Is that correct?"

A. "Yes."

Q. "And you also tried to give him some insight into some of these problems in that he may not be perceiving the whole truth of the situation here, and you wanted him to put that in perspective; is that correct?"

A. "Yes. I tried to give him those kinds of suggestions, I'm not sure he heard me at all."

Q. "And that meant in reality, to put it in reality; is that correct?"

A. "Yes."

10.3 Cross-Examination of Dr. Binger in the Alger Hiss Trial

The following extensive extract of an historical transcript, from the Alger Hiss perjury trial of 1950, demonstrates that the techniques and areas of cross-examination of a psychiatrist or psychologist do not change.

Alger Hiss was a Harvard-educated, well-connected government lawyer and State Department official during the Roosevelt administration. Whitaker Chambers, from a working-class background, was a writer and editor. Chambers left the Communist Party and, when he was questioned by the House Un-American Activities Committee (HUAC), he accused Hiss of committing espionage for the Communists. Hiss denied the claim, but a grand jury indicted Hiss for perjury after the statute of limitations for espionage had run out. Chambers had hidden some microfilm he obtained from Hiss in a hollow pumpkin, which were famously known as the "Pumpkin Papers," and he also had other documents from the State Department, which he claimed Hiss had passed to him.

In the first trial, the jury was hung. The second trial featured a new defense witness, Dr. Carl Binger, a seemingly qualified psychiatrist with a national reputation. Dr. Binger, in response to a hypothetical question on direct examination, opined that Whitaker Chambers was a psychopathic personality and a pathological liar. Thomas Murphy, the lead prosecutor in both trials, conducted the cross-examination. The areas of cross-examination previously discussed in this book are highlighted.

Putting Condition in Perspective

Q. "Did you explain the fact that Mr. Chambers, for instance, had these four handwritten notes, which notes contained sometimes copies, sometimes extracts, from State Department telegrams that had passed over Mr. Hiss's desk? Did you explain that?"

A. "No, sir, I did not."

. . .

Delay in Board Certification

Q. "My question was, did you tell us on your direct examination when it was in fact that you were certified? Do you recall?"

A. "I said that I was certified by the American Board of Neurology and Psychiatry."

Q. "Did you tell us what year that was?"

A. "No, I did not."

Q. "Would 1946 be approximately correct?"

A. "Yes. I can explain that here if you want me to."

Q. "Let me see, doctor, you graduated from medical school in 1914?"

A. "I did."

Q. "And you were therefore certified as a psychiatrist 32 years later?"

A. "That is correct."

Not Admitted into Professional Society

Q. "Now, were you ever refused admission as a member of the American Psychiatric Association for reasons of insufficiency of training in psychiatry?"

A. "I think the facts are these; I applied for admission in the American Psychiatric Association—"

Q. "Could you, doctor, try to answer the question just yes or no? Your counsel will have the opportunity on redirect."

A. "I can't answer it yes or no because I do not know the actual facts. I know that there was a regulation in the American Psychiatric Association that to be a member—"

Q. "Now, please, doctor, I am going to ask you if you can't answer the question yes or no perhaps we can go to something else. The question is, to your knowledge were you ever refused admission as a member of this Association of Psychiatrists by reason of lack of experience as a psychiatrist in psychiatry, yes or no?"

A. "I don't know the exact answer. I know that my membership was deferred for a year. Whether I was actually refused, I don't know."

Q. "Well, do you know, for instance, whether your membership was deferred, as you put it, more than once?"

A. "My impression is that it was once. It may have been more than once."

Lack of Qualifications

Q. "Now, doctor, what full-time training in an institution devoted to the study of anatomy or pathology of the brain have you had?"

A. "None."

Q. "Doctor, you also said in your direct examination that you were an associate professor of clinical psychiatry at Cornell. Does that mean, doctor, that you teach a class of students each day?"

Not Full-Time Professor

A. "No, sir, not each day. The title "clinical psychiatry" means I am on part time."

Q. "You are on what, sir?"

A. "On part time, not on full time."

Lack of Full-Time Teaching

Q. "And how many classes a month or a year did you teach in clinical psychiatry since that time?"

A. "My duties are variegated. Sometimes I have two classes a week; sometimes only one class a week."

Q. "And consisting, say, of an hour each?"

A. "An hour and a half."

Lack of Graduate Study

Q. "Now, you said that after you had been with the Rockefeller Foundation you had gone to Europe and you studied, I think you said, in Zurich, Heidelberg and London?"

A. "That is right."

Q. "How long did you study, doctor, in those places?"

A. "Well, I was gone all together 18 months, and the 18 months were distributed mostly between Heidelberg, Zurich and London."

. . .

Q. "What I was trying to find out, doctor, was the amount of time that you devoted in these foreign cities to the study of psychiatry?"

A. "That is right, about half and half in Heidelberg."

Q. "Were you studying there, doctor, or were you under treatment?"

A. "I was studying and I was being treated in the sense that anybody who studies psychiatry has to be examined by Dr. Jung."

Q. "Other than being treated by Dr. Jung, have you ever been psychoanalyzed by anybody else?"

A. "Certainly. Nobody can do psychoanalysis without having been psychoanalyzed."

Q. "Would you try, doctor, just to say yes or no, and we will go much faster?"

A. "Okay."

Q. "How many times have you been psychoanalyzed?"

A. "Once by Dr. Jung and once here in New York."

Q. "Do you have a copy of the findings?"

A. "No."

(This is an historically interesting question and somewhat humorous. With the decrease in psychoanalysts, there will not be much opportunity to inquire in this area.)

Q. "Now, were those the only places, London, Zurich and Heidelberg, where you studied—you didn't tell us how long you studied psychiatry in London?"

A. "In London it was partly psychiatry and partly medicine."

Q. "Half and half?"

A. "About half and half. I was in London about four or five months; I can't remember."

Q. "And you would estimate that half is devoted to medicine and half to psychiatry?"

A. "Psychiatry and neurology."

Q. "Well, does that comprise the different countries that you were in Europe at that time, Switzerland, Germany and England?"

A. "For study. The rest was travel."

Q. "Did you devote much time to travel in other places?"

A. "About a month in Italy."

Q. "Is that all?"

A. "I went to the Isle of Wight for a few weeks, but I was there mostly for work with just a short vacation here and there."

Q. "Any other traveling at all; specifically any worthwhile time at all?"

A. "On that trip?"

Q. "Yes."

A. "Of course I have traveled at other times. You mean—"

Q. "I think you said you were abroad about 18 months?"

A. "That is right. A week or so in Czechoslovakia."

Q. "Any place else?"

A. "Germany, Switzerland, Italy, England, Czechoslovakia. That is all I can recall now."

Q. "Belgium?"

A. "No."

Q. "Denmark?"

A. "No, sir."

Q. "Do you remember on your passport application what you told the State Department as to what countries you wanted to see, go to?"

A. "I have not the faintest idea what I told them, but those are the only places I went."

Q. "You can't remember what you put on your application?"

A. "That was in 1928. I can't remember."

Q. "You can't remember?"

A. "No. I know I wasn't in Denmark. I have never been in Denmark."

. . .

Q. "But I was just touching the part about the passport application. You can't recall what you said on your passport application as to what countries you intended to visit?"

A. "I cannot."

Lack of Residency Training

Q. "Now, doctor, you said you did some work or were attached—I forget the phrase you used—at the Vanderbilt Clinic? Does that mean you were a resident there, or is that how you worked in that—?"

A. "That Clinic is an out-patient clinic. One can't be a resident."

Q. "How about the Psychiatric Institute? Was that a residency there, too?"

A. "I was not a resident there.

Q. "That was an out-patient department?"

A. "Out patient."

Q. "How about the Cornell? Out patient, too?"

A. "Well, at the old Cornell Clinic that was also [an] out-patient department. In the Paine-Whitney I have also had an appointment in the house."

Putting Condition in Perspective

Q. "So that we can go to something else, you have never spent any full-time residency in a mental institution at all?"

A. "That is right."

Q. "Doctor, so that we can understand, psychotic is the word that doctors use for what we lay people call insane?"

A. "Yes, that is right."

Q. "You don't say that Mr. Chambers is insane, do you?"

A. "I say that he is not insane."

. . .

Q. "Well, the question was, doctor, can you form a complete opinion of the personality of a person by merely observing him or her on a witness chair?"

A. "Of course not."

Lack of Prior History

Q. "Now, doctor, would it help at all to a psychiatrist such as yourself in forming a professional opinion, a professional psychiatric opinion of a person's personality, to have detailed information concerning that person's early childhood? For instance, his or her relationship with parents, the relationship with brothers and sisters, in the early formative years? Is that important, doctor, when you, as a psychiatrist, are going to form an opinion as to a person's personality?"

A. "Certainly."

Q. "You didn't have any of that in this case, did you, doctor?"

A. "Not as much as I would have liked to have had."

Q. "And you did tell us that it sometimes is important to have this other information about the early associations of the child with his parents and with his brothers and sisters, playmates, and a great deal, I suppose, doctor, of the person's private information; does that also help, doctor, to have that information?"

A. "The more information one has, the better."

Q. "Well, can we say the less information a person has, the worse?"

A. "Certainly."

Attacking Opinion: Psychiatry Not an Exact Science—Have You Ever Been Wrong?

Q. "Talking about other psychiatrists, doctor, would you say that other psychiatrists, let us say as qualified as yourself, might perhaps have a different opinion based upon the facts that you have here?"

A. "I should be very surprised if they did. I have talked to a great many of them."

Q. "Well, whether you would be surprised or not, doctor, what is your answer to the question? Would you say that perhaps another qualified psychiatrist would have a different opinion than you do?"

A. "Well, it could be, naturally. That is something I don't know about."

Q. "Well, the science of medicine and psychiatry is not quite an exact science, is it, doctor?"

A. "Of course, not."

Q. "And doctors have been known to disagree on diagnoses?"

A. "Frequently."

Q. "And some doctors have been known to be wrong on diagnoses?"

A. "Frequently."

Q. "Have you ever been wrong, doctor?"

A. "Certainly."

Q. "Now doctor, have you in the years since you graduated from medical school testified in a courtroom concerning a witness's personality, other than this time?

Lack of Testifying Before on This Specific Issue

A. "Well, if you include in the word personality his mental and emotional health, I would say yes."

Q. "Doctor, I wanted to find out whether or not you have testified in a courtroom concerning a witness's personality. Now, that term is your term. You said that Mr. Chambers had a psychopathic personality. Now, have you ever testified in a courtroom concerning a person, a witness, and told that jury that he had or she had or didn't have a psychopathic personality?"

A. "In those terms, no."

Q. "Now, doctor, as an experienced psychiatrist would you say that a person who in your opinion would be a psychopathic personality would never tell the truth at any time?"

Standard Psychological Fact

A. "I wouldn't say that."

Q. "In other words, even a person with a psychopathic personality would sometimes tell the truth?"

A. "Yes, if his particular emotions were not involved he could."

Q. "In other words, you can't tell, as you told us before, which part is true and which part is false, and you do not say as a doctor that everything a psychopath says is a lie; that is correct; isn't it?"

A. "You are right. That is right."

Motive for Testifying

Q. "How long have you known either of the Hisses?"

A. "The first time I ever saw either of them was October 15, 1947."

Q. "Your wife's name is—what is your wife's first name?"

A. "Clarinda."

Q. "Does she teach?"

A. "She is the assistant to the head mistress at Dalton School."

Q. "And that is the same Dalton School that Mrs. Hiss used to teach at?"

A. "That is correct."

Q. "And your wife is a graduate of what college?"

A. "Bryn Mawr."

Q. "Bryn Mawr?"

A. "That is right."

Q. "You are a graduate of Harvard?"

A. "I am."

Q. "And your wife Bryn Mawr?"

A. "That is right."

Q. "Do you know what college or law school Mr. Hiss went to?"

A. "Yes. He went to Harvard Law School."

Q. "And his wife?"

A. "Bryn Mawr."

Q. "I see. Now, doctor, you told the jury at the last trial that you were testifying at that time, when you were asked a hypothetical question, without fee; do you recall that?"

A. "I so do."

. . .

Psychological Text Cross-Examination; Lack of Firm Diagnostic Criteria

Q. "Would you say, doctor, and again not being disrespectful, that the phrase is, in substance, sort of a wastepaper basket classification of a lot of symptoms? In other words, they can't agree, doctors can't agree as to what all of this represents and they sort of get a catchall phrase, a wastepaper basket classification and drop it right there and say that is a psychopathic personality?"

A. "I think that is fair, if you will let me say that in that wastepaper basket are put people who behave in a certain characteristic way."

Q. "If you are willing to accept that classification, doctor, you are not willing, however, to accept the characterization 'vague'? In other words, you are willing to say that perhaps it can be classified as a wastepaper basket classification, but it is not vague?"

A. "Well, that is good, that is a good point. I think that psychiatric diagnosis has a certain vagueness, with some exceptions. I would include vagueness as related to psychopathic personality, yes."

. . .

Q. "Doctor, tell me whether you agree with Dr. Preu. He says: 'The present status of the concept of psychopathic personality is highly unsatisfactory.' . . . And in the conclusion he says: '. . . The term 'psychopathic personality', as commonly understood, is useless in psychiatric research. It is a diagnosis of convenience arrived at by a process of exclusion. It does not refer to a specific behavioral entity. It serves as a scrap-basket to which is relegated a group of otherwise, unclassified personality disorders and problems.' And do you agree with that statement, doctor?"

A. "Yes, with every word of it. I think it is excellent."

. . .

Basis of Opinion Stronger with Missing Prior History

Q. "What I am trying to prove, to get it right down to simple terms, is that the basis for your expert opinion is not a warranted basis for an expert opinion; in other words, that you didn't have enough information here to form an honest, intelligent psychiatric opinion. That is what I am trying to prove. I am asking you whether or not if you had this additional information you wouldn't be better qualified. Won't you concede that?"

A. "I won't concede that I did not have the basis of an honest and intelligent opinion, because I wouldn't have given it had I not thought it both honest and intelligent."

Q. "Wouldn't you have a better basis, wouldn't you be more qualified, wouldn't you feel stronger in your own mind?"

A. "I would feel much stronger in my own mind if he came to see me as a patient for cure and treatment; much."

Q. "Wouldn't you feel better, whether Mr. Chambers came to you or not, if you were supplied in your hypothetical question with all the information you wanted concerning the patient's first 16 years of life?"

A. "I would welcome more, yes."

Q. "And wouldn't you feel more qualified then in expressing an opinion with that information?"

A. "I would feel better qualified than I am now, yes."

Cross-Examination on Own Writings

Q. "Do you agree, doctor, with the statement by a doctor who said: 'To be sure, psychiatric investigation takes into consideration all bodily abnormalities of form and function, and no examination would be regarded as complete without careful physical studies as well'. Do you agree with that?"

A. "As regards patients who are to be treated, yes."

Q. "With regard to giving testimony in court: No?"

A. "In the case of psychopathic personality there are one or two physical facts that are important."

Q. "Doctor, some doctor said this and I am trying to find out whether you agree with him: 'To be sure, psychiatric investigation takes into consideration all bodily abnormalities of form and function, and no examination would be regarded as complete without careful physical studies as well.' Don't you agree with that, doctor?"

A. "Certainly as regards patients."

Q. "You said it yourself, didn't you?"

A. "I don't recall. I have said an awful lot in my day."

Q. "You have said an awful lot—what?"

A. "I said I have said and written an awful lot, and I may have said that. You probably know that I have."

Attacking Opinion—Breaking Down Symptoms

Q. "Now, doctor, when you started to describe the different symptoms of a person with a psychopathic personality you ran through 12 or so, and you said chronic, persistent and repetitive lying; stealing, deception; alcoholism and drug addiction; abnormal sexuality, vagabondage, panhandling. For our purposes, doctor, we can eliminate immediately three of those, can't we—drug addiction, alcoholism and sexual abnormality? There is nothing in the hypothetical question that you have that even touches on any of those?"

A. "That is right."

Q. "Right. So that we have—the first one I think you talked about when you started to outline the characteristics was the lying, the repetitive lying pattern. Doctor, let me ask you, do people who lie necessarily give to a psychiatrist a symptom of a psychopathic personality just by lying?"

. . .

A. "Isolated lie, isolated any event would mean nothing."

Q. "Let us suppose an occasional lie to your wife?"

A. "Pardon?"

Q. "Would it indicate a symptom of a psychopathic personality?"

A. "I wouldn't say so."

Q. "Let us suppose, doctor, a taxpayer lied a little bit in his income tax return. What do you think that would indicate? A symptom of psychopathic personality?"

A. "It could indicate a symptom. There would be an awful lot of psychopaths if that were the criterion."

Q. "Supposing, doctor, you were stopped by a policeman who said that you were speeding; you told him that you had a hurry call for a patient, had to get there by a certain time, and you lied a little bit and you ended up with no ticket, no ticket. Would that indicate a symptom of a psychopathic personality?"

A. "Certainly not."

Q. "Well, let us suppose that some of us tell our children that there is a Santa Claus and continue that statement to children over a period of years until they are adolescent. Would you say that that indicates on the part of the parents a symptom of psychopathic personality?"

A. "No, I wouldn't."

Q. "How about lying to your wife to avoid an unpleasant argument?"

A. "Pretty normal."

Q. "Normal?"

A. "Pretty normal performance."

Q. "Some lying is normal, doctor?

A. "In the sense of statistically normal, yes. It is undesirable, I think."

Q. "Would you say, doctor, that the taking of anything that is not yours is some evidence of psychopathic personality?"

A. "Well, you gave a very good example of taking a piece of bread when you were hungry. I don't think that is—"

Q. "Did you ever take a hotel towel or a Pullman towel?"

A. "I couldn't swear that I had or hadn't. I don't think so."

Q. "Well, if you did, doctor, or if one of the jurors did, would you say that was evidence of a symptom of psychopathic personality?"

A. "It would have no bearing on it."

Q. "It would have no bearing?"

A. "No."

Q. "Now, doctor, you also described as one of the characteristics the trait of insensibility to the feelings of others; that that is one of the characteristics of a person who has a psychopathic personality; and I think you cited the play that Mr. Chambers wrote in college called *Play for Puppets* and I think you said, doctor, that the reason that that was a symptom was that it showed—I am not too sure of the phrase—a disregard for the feelings of Christians; that it offended them; isn't that what you said?"

A. "Well, it seemed to have offended them."

Q. "Sorry, sir?"

A. "It seemed to have offended them because he was asked to leave Columbia as the result of it."

Q. "And I think Mr. Chambers himself said on the stand that he thought it was a highly insulting piece of work; did you assume that?"

A. "That was not in the hypothetical question."

Q. "I think he said it was highly offensive. Doctor, do you feel that anybody who does or says anything that might be taken by others as offensive is a symptom of psychopathic personality?"

A. "No, we all do that all the time."

Q. "Would you say that in order to classify it as a symptom it has to have a real purpose, to be offensive?"

A. "No, it has to have a certain callousness, a certain obvious lack of consideration for the kind of feelings that most people would appreciate."

Q. "Well, doctor, do you say, for instance, that Anatole France was a psychopathic personality?"

A. "I have never made a study of him."

Q. "Well, you have read some of his books, haven't you, doctor?"

A. "Two things I have read: *Penguin Island*—"

Q. "Well, let us take *Penguin Island*—?"

A. "I don't know it well enough to have any real idea."

Q. "Don't you think that was pretty offensive to certain types of religious people?"

A. "I am sure it was."

Q. "And would you say, therefore, that he, Anatole France, was a psychopathic personality because of that?"

A. "I do not make a diagnosis on one piece of evidence. If I knew all the rest of Anatole France's life I might have some view, but I do not, and I have no opportunity of finding out."

Q. "Well, are you familiar with what Profession Van Doren thought about the play?"

A. "Well, that is not in the hypothetical question."

Q. "No, but are you familiar with it?"

A. "I think he thought it was pretty clever."

Q. "Very brilliant, wasn't it?"

A. "I don't remember the word 'brilliant'. You tell me, I will be glad to hear."

Q. "Well, doctor, can we say that reading a play or a book by someone helps you to determine whether or not they are psychopathic? Can you tell from reading a play or book whether the author is psychopathic?"

A. "Not from that alone, certainly not."

Q. "Not from that alone?"

A. "Certainly not."

Q. "Well, doctor, would you say a person who said this was insensitive of the feelings of others: 'Our Catholic subjects are relatively happy, free from neurotic symptoms, blissfully self-deceived, superficial in their psychological discernments, always competent to clothe raw facts in the rational vestments of their faith. In these respects the Jewish subjects were outstandingly different. Most of them were highly self-conscious, relatively insecure, burdened by neurotic complexes; painfully aware of disturbing impulses and feelings, psychologically penetrating, and unusually quick to comprehend (and often to accept) even the least flattering interpretations of their behavior. They were not contained by their religion and they never made use of its symbolism in depicting their difficulties.' Would you say that would be offensive to certain types of people?"

A. "I don't see why it should be."

Q. "You don't think so?"

A. "No."

Q. "Do you know who said it?"

A. "No."

Q. "Dr. Murray. Now, would you say that this phrase would be insensitive to the feelings of others, that 'Every really good wife is partly mother, sister, psychiatric nurse and courtesan'?"

A. "Would I say that was offensive?"

Q. "Yes, that the person who said that was insensitive to the feelings of others, to call a woman both a mother and a prostitute?"

A. "Well, since I said that myself I could hardly say it was offensive."

Q. "You don't think that that is an exhibition of insensitivity to the feelings of others?"

A. "I certainly do not, because I think it is the truth."

Q. "Would you say that when Mr. Chambers, testifying in the House Committee, said: 'The story has spread that in testifying against Mr. Hiss I am working out some old grudge or motives of revenge or hatred. I do not hate Mr. Hiss. We were close friends but we were caught in the tragedy of history. Mr. Hiss represents the concealed enemy against which we are all fighting and I am fighting. I have testified against him with remorse and pity, but in the moment of history in which the nation now stands, so help me God, I could not do otherwise.' Would you say, doctor, that that was a statement of someone who has a certain insensitivity to the feelings of others?"

A. "I think it is a statement that reflects a certain kind of grandiosity which we find in others of his statements."

Q. "My question was, does it convey to you, as an experienced doctor, the impression that there was a man who was insensitive to the feelings of others?"

A. "If that were a sincere statement I would say no."

Q. "You have no evidence, doctor, that you rely on, have you, that it was insincere?"

A. "No."

Q. "Doctor, when you said that one of the things that you considered as a symptom of this insensitivity to the feelings of others was the fact that Mr. Chambers lived in an illicit relationship with Ida Dailes, and that he took her to the home of his mother—did you know, doctor, as part of your assumed state of facts that at that time each, Mr. Chambers and Ida Dailes, were each Communists—did you know that?"

A. "I did."

Q. "And did you know that the testimony was that Communists at that time thought that marriage was a bourgeois convention? Was that part of your assumed state of facts?"

A. "Was his mother also a Communist?"

Q. "Perhaps you didn't hear my question, doctor—did you?"

A. "I did. But the insensitivity—"

Q. "The question is, did you know that at that time Communists thought that marriage was a bourgeois convention?"

A. "Did I know that?"

Q. "Yes."

A. "I did know it."

Q. "As part of your assumed state of facts?"

A. "Yes, that is right."

Q. "And did you know further that the bringing of that woman to the home of his mother was his mother's request, she having said that she had lost one son by suicide and she did not want to lose another; did you know that, doctor, when you said that that was one of the evidences of the insensitivity to the feelings of others?"

A. "If it was at his mother's request I would not say so."

Q. "And, doctor, don't you know too—did you form an opinion, doctor, because of the fact that they were living together, just by itself, as man and wife?"

A. "No."

Q. "That was condoned by the State of New York, wasn't it, at that time?"

A. "That I don't happen to know."

Q. "Well, common law marriages were accepted as part of the law of this land, and still are in many states."

A. "I am not very conversant with the law. I am willing to take any statement you make about it as true."

Q. "Well, you have heard in your talks with others of such a thing as common law marriages?"

A. "Yes."

Q. "Would you consider, doctor, the actions of Mr. Chambers in resigning from his job at *Time* and giving up a $30,000-a-year job, assuming, doctor, that he did that because he did not want to hurt the people with whom he was associated, or hurt the magazine itself, didn't want to embarrass them, and he did it voluntarily, that that was evidence of a man who was insensitive to the feelings of others?"

A. "If you ask me to make the assumption?"

Q. "Yes, assuming that is true, doctor?"

A. "No, then I would not."

Q. "What other acts, doctor, did you assume in your state of facts to come to the conclusion that Mr. Chambers evidenced symptoms of insensitivity to the feelings of others other than the play, *The Play for Puppets*, and this Ida Dailes incident?"

A. "Just those two."

Q. "Just those two?"

A. "Yes."

Q. "And if you assume that he went to the home of his mother at his mother's request, you would have just *The Play for Puppets*?"

A. "That is correct."

. . .

Q. "Doctor, did you say that the only criterion you have to determine whether a person is a psychopathic personality is whether a person's behavior is bizarre or queer?"

A. "I said nothing like that. I said that about behavior, about bizarre behavior."

Q. "In other words, that is an accurate definition of bizarre behavior as distinguished from a definition of a psychopath?"

A. "That is no definition of bizarre behavior. I said the test we have of bizarre behavior is to compare it with the behavior of ourselves and other ordinary people."

Q. "On page 3680."

A. "Bizarre behavior and impulsive acts, yes, sir. May I define what I mean by that?"

Q. "Yes."

A. "By bizarre behavior I mean strange, queer behavior, behavior that the ordinary person does not indulge in. That is the real test we have for what is strange and what is queer. Does it seem reasonable and plausible?"

Q. "That is what you said, doctor?"

A. "Yes, but that is not the question you just asked me."

Q. "Yes. I did it wrong. You were defining bizarre behavior?"

A. "That is correct."

Q. "Doctor, you said that in determining what is an example of bizarre behavior is whether or not the reasonable person does it; isn't that the test more or less?"

A. "That is pretty much it, yes."

Q. "Now, the living in a common law relationship with Ida Dailes—is that bizarre? Was it bizarre?"

A. “I wouldn’t say so.”

Q. “I think you said that leaving Williams College impulsively was bizarre.”

A. “I think leaving on a night train after having been there two days and suddenly changing your mind is certainly not very reasonable or deliberate or the way you would expect a more rational person to behave. That alone is not a conspicuous example of it.”

Q. “Well, is it bizarre, doctor, under your definition?”

A. “Relatively.”

Q. “Relatively?”

A. “Yes.”

Q. “When you testified you said that he left—I think you said he left impulsively. Did you assume that as one of the facts, that he left impulsively?”

A. “Yes.”

Q. “Doctor, assuming that it was two or three days, and that his roommate had bought some secondhand furniture to furnish their room, and then one evening there was a sort of a freshman dinner to which they each were invited, and he told his roommate that he did not want to go, that he had a problem that he had to think out, and he did not, in fact, go; he told his roommate that he was going to consult the Scriptures—would that be bizarre behavior up to that point?”

A. “No.”

Q. "Of course not. Reading the Scriptures would not be bizarre, would it?"

A. "Well, to a man who thinks of himself as an atheist it might be, but certainly not ordinarily."

Q. "Well, doctor, this was in the beginning of his college career?"

A. "Yes."

Q. "Did you assume that he was an atheist then?"

A. "No."

Q. "So that reading the Bible in an attempt to solve a problem, you do not consider bizarre?"

A. "No, it might be quite the reverse."

Q. "What is the reverse of bizarre?"

A. "Sensible."

Q. "Sensible?"

A. "Yes."

Q. "And you said that what was bizarre was the fact that he left at midnight to catch a midnight train. Do all people who catch midnight trains, doctor, exhibit bizarre behavior at all?"

A. "They could. They don't need to necessarily. It depends upon why they do it."

Q. "Doctor, you have been in the Grand Central at midnight, haven't you?"

A. "Yes."

Q. "All those people running and scurrying for trains, you would not ascribe to them bizarre behavior?"

A. "I wouldn't have any idea what the meaning of their behavior was."

Q. "Doctor, if a train left at midnight to go to New York and he got on the midnight train, isn't that what any reasonable person would do?"

A. "Yes, if the train left at midnight and he got there at one o'clock it might be bizarre behavior."

Q. "Doctor, the testimony is that he got a midnight train; nothing bizarre about that by itself, is there?"

A. "Nothing whatever."

Q. "And I think you said that one who consults the Bible—I think George Washington consulted the Bible at Valley Forge when he had a problem, didn't he?"

A. "That is correct."

Q. "Now, what you did describe as bizarre, doctor, was the giving of rather important papers, Mr. Chambers handing over important papers to his wife's nephew, whereas the ordinary, reasonable, normal person would have put them in a bank. Did you know, doctor, or did you assume that that person who received the papers was an attorney practicing here in New York City and a relative of Mr. Chambers? Did you know that the papers were handed to him?"

A. "At that time he was an attorney?"

Q. "Yes."

A. "I have heard that he was a lawyer."

Q. "In describing the actions as bizarre do you say now that the giving of valuable papers to an attorney and telling the attorney to keep these in a safe place, 'and if anything happens to me, disclose them'—is that bizarre behavior, doctor?"

A. "I think one has to take into account the nature of the papers, what was involved in the papers; and also the fact that he then testified that he had forgotten about their existence."

Q. "Well, let us treat each separately, doctor, if we can. Do you say to this Court and jury that when a person gives papers that he attaches value or significance to to an attorney, and the attorney is also a relative, that that fact manifests bizarre behavior?"

A. "Not on that assumption, no."

Q. "So that it is consistent with those people who would put it in a bank to give it to an attorney?"

A. "Of course, you are asking me to assume part of the trust and not all of the truth. But in so far as you have gone—"

Q. "Wait a minute, doctor. I did not know that you were able to tell which was part of the truth and which was not part of the truth."

A. "By 'truth' I mean what I have been asked to assume in the hypothetical question."

Q. "Doctor, assuming that the testimony in this case shows that Mr. Chambers sometime in 1938 gave some of these papers that are in evidence here to his wife's nephew, who was a duly licensed practicing attorney in this city, with instructions to keep them for safekeeping, and if anything happened to him to disclose their contents—now, as far as I have gone I think you have to agree with me, doctor, that that is not bizarre behavior?"

A. "I do agree with you."

Q. "Now, doctor, you said another exhibition of bizarre behavior was the putting of the microfilm, the developed strip and the undeveloped films in a pumpkin. Can you think of any similar act during our American history where somebody else did a somewhat similar thing?"

A. "No. You will have to tell me. I can't remember."

Q. "Do you remember, doctor, during the Revolutionary times when they put the charter in the charter oak up in Hartford to hide it from the British?"

A. "Yes, I do."

Q. "Were the actions of those people at that time bizarre in hiding it in a tree, just an old paper?"

A. "Well, that was a very primitive community and in older times, and they did not have repositories for valuable documents, and I can see the analogy but I still regard hollowing out a pumpkin and putting microfilms in it as sufficiently bizarre so that when I read about it I was immediately arrested by the fact, as were a great many other people, because it is not the way a modern twentieth century human being, even living on a farm, usually behaves."

Q. "If, doctor, you assume that these microfilms were previously in his house and he moved them from room to room, and that the day that he put them in the pumpkin was the day that he was going to leave his farm, and assume further that there were different people in and about the farm looking for things, wouldn't you say, doctor, that that was a pretty good hiding place?"

A. "It was."

Q. "No matter how bizarre it was?"

A. "It certainly was a good hiding place, yes."

Q. "All right. As a matter of fact, don't you remember reading, doctor, that when Benedict Arnold sold out West Point and gave the plans to Major Andre, do you know where he put the plans when he was caught, just up here by Tarrytown?"

A. "No, I don't."

Q. "He had them in the boot of his shoe, the sole of his boot. Was that bizarre on the part of an intelligent British officer?"

A. "No, I wouldn't say so."

Q. "Well, how about the mother of Moses hiding the little child in the bulrushes? Was that bizarre?"

A. "Well, she could hardly put it in a safe deposit vault."

Q. "Now, doctor, you don't tell us that all things that don't fit in safe deposit boxes are therefore bizarre, do you?"

A. "No, I don't."

Q. "I am asking you, doctor, whether the action of Moses' mother in putting the young child in the bulrushes was bizarre behavior?"

A. "I don't know the circumstances and I wouldn't know where else she had to hide the child. If that was the only place, it certainly was not bizarre."

Q. "You know what her fear was, don't you?"

A. "Yes."

Q. "There was an edict out to kill all Hebrew children."

A. "That is right."

Q. "Now, doctor, I have made an analysis of all of the testimony that Mr. Chambers gave at the last trial and on the one day when you were present at this trial and I find that—I have the statistics right here—I find, doctor, that those phrases that you have told us, 'must have been,' 'should have been,' 'would have been,' in 717 pages of testimony come to a total of ten, ten times. Now my recollection is that Mr. Chambers answered very responsively, very quickly, without hesitation, and nevertheless you say that our observation on those days, you observed that he used these phrases repeatedly; and an actual count in 717 pages, doctor, discloses ten times. For instance, he said 'my daughter was born [in] 1933, so she must have been about a year old'—" Now, doctor, do you say that a person who uses phrases similar to that gives evidence of a bizarre behavior?"

A. "I did not use that in connection with bizarre behavior at all. I used it in connection with the particular kind of memory that Mr. Chambers revealed."

Q. "Ten times in 717 pages. Do you know how many times Mr. Hiss used similar phrases in 500 pages?"

A. "I haven't any idea; I didn't hear him testify."

Q. "Well, I have some statistics on that and ask you—"

Mr. Cross: "Now, if your Honor please, I submit—I did not object to Mr. Murphy reciting what Mr. Chambers testified to at the first trial. This is not proper cross-examination, to have read into the record testimony at the earlier trial. It would simply mean prolonging the trial to count up various statements of witnesses. And there has been no evidence whatever with reference to Mr. Hiss, nor his testimony at the first trial, except as Mr. Murphy asked him when he was on the stand. So—"

The Court: "I think this is for the purpose of making comparisons between an alleged normal person and an alleged abnormal person. I think it is proper."

Q. "So that there will be no confusion, I am talking about Mr. Hiss's testimony at this trial, and the Judge permitted you, doctor, to testify as to your observations at the last trial. So I am now coming to whether you have any idea about the number of times that Mr. Hiss, in 500 and some-odd pages, used phrases similar to that. My computation, doctor, is in 590 pages Mr. Hiss used a phrase like that or similar 158 times. Now, do you form any conclusions, doctor, by the use of phrases?"

A. "No."

Q. "You did describe as bizarre behavior the meeting of Mr. Wadleigh at Jackson Place back in 1939? Do you remember that part of the question, doctor?"

A. "Yes, that was described as a stone's throw from the State Department."

Q. "Yes, it is the next street away."

A. "Yes."

Q. "Did you in your diagnosis of that as bizarre behavior—did you realize that that was in 1939, a year after Mr. Chambers had broken with the Party and he was then not in the underground?"

A. "I don't think I took that into consideration."

Q. "If you assumed those to be the facts, doctor, would you still describe that as bizarre?"

A. "Not necessarily, no."

. . .

Q. "Yes. I can think of another person who had fear, a man named Trotsky. Do you remember the fear that he must have had?"

A. "That is right."

Q. "Now, doctor, is a person who breaks with the Party and who goes into hiding, is that fact itself, that of just going into hiding after you have left the Party, is that evidence of a psychopathic personality?"

A. "No, certainly not."

Q. "Doctor, a person who is in hiding and wants to come out of hiding has to take the first step somewhere; so isn't there a distinction, doctor, between being in hiding and being vigilant, careful?"

A. "Yes; he testified he was in hiding for a year I believe."

Q. "Assuming, doctor, that the facts are that the actual hiding was for a short period of time in a little country road outside of Baltimore, and for another short period of time, I think a month, in Daytona Beach,

Florida, and then there was a gradual lifting—a buying of a house in his name and him coming to New York to get work to live on, but at the same time vigilant. Would you say that those were bizarre actions of a person who had only recently broken with the Communist Party?"

A. "Do you want me to assume what you have just said to be true?"

Q. "If you will, doctor."

A. "Then I do not think it is bizarre."

. . .

Q. "You sort of saw a symbolism, too, I think in the fact that Mr. Chambers went underground, and I think the symbolism that you said you saw was that that was a symbol of the brother's burial—he went underground—and it sort of symbolized in his mind the brother's burial?"

A. "That is not what I meant."

Q. "Well, will you tell us what you said or what you meant?"

A. "I will tell you what I meant. Taking into consideration this particular kind of reaction after his brother's death, taking into consideration the poem in which motionlessness and death and reunion are implied, he then became a fanatical Communist—Chambers—and went underground. I said, to your amusement, because I saw you smile when I said it, that was a kind of symbolic burial of himself; the brother was dead and he buried himself in the Communist underground. That is exactly what I said and meant."

Q. "And did you say you said it because you wanted to amuse me? Is that what you said?"

A. "Oh no. I said you seemed to be amused that I made that remark. I was not trying to amuse you. I am not here for that."

Q. "Well, doctor, don't you assume in your state of facts that the brother was buried underground?"

A. "I don't know where the brother was buried."

Q. "Why of course. Suppose the brother was cremated? What would be the symbolic symbol there?"

A. "I don't think it is quite—I don't think that is quite as literal as that, Mr. Murphy. We speak of burying in the Communist underground, going underground. Usually after a person dies there is the thought of burial. Now, whether the brother was cremated or whether his ashes were scattered on the four winds has nothing to do with my assumption. It was an assumption, I still make it, and it can be given whatever importance you wish to give it."

Q. "Well, doctor, let us suppose that you assumed that he did not go underground as a Communist functionary until three years I think it was, some five years later?"

A. "Yes, I know there was an interval. He did say however that he became a fanatical Communist after his brother's death."

Q. "But tell us about the symbolism of going underground five years later pursuant to orders from his superior—do you attach some significance to that in connection with the proposed death with that intervening time there and pursuant to orders?"

A. "I think the Unconscious recognizes no statute of limitations. I think this is a continuous process that goes on in the mind, and whether it is one year or five years or ten years has nothing to do with it."

Q. "Doctor, if he did it pursuant to orders, pursuant to the orders of his superior and went underground—"

A. "He accepted those orders, didn't he?"

Q. "Yes, assuming he did it pursuant to orders, do you still attach this symbolism to it and tie it in in some way with the proposed death?"

A. "I am not trying to lay too much emphasis on it. I think it is a significant fact worth bearing in mind."

Q. "Doctor, you said that another characteristic was false accusations, and you gave as an example the fact that Mr. Chambers falsely accused Mr. Duggan. Now, doctor, assuming now that Mr. Chambers did not accuse Mr. Duggan of being a member of the Communist Party when he spoke to Mr. Berle in 1939, what other evidence would you have in your hypothetical question that there was evidence of false accusations with regard to Mr. Duggan?"

A. "With regard to Mr. Duggan?"

Q. "Yes."

A. "Oh, none."

Q. "None?"

A. "It is based entirely on that."

Q. "Because your assumed state of facts said that when he talked with Mr. Murphy in 1945 and 1946 he specifically said Mr. Duggan was not a member of the Party."

A. "Yes; I was asked to assume that he had said that to Mr. Berle, and then that he had reversed himself."

Q. "But I am saying, doctor, if you assume that he did not in fact say that to Mr. Berle and said the opposite to Mr. Murphy, and said so in so many words when here on the stand, you would say that there was no evidence as far as Mr. Duggan was concerned of false accusations; that is right, isn't it?"

A. "That is correct."

Q. "And you know, of course, that the statement with regard to Mr. Duggan that appears in Mr. Berle's notes was Mr. Berle's notes that he gave to the FBI in 1943; there is no testimony there that Mr. Duggan was accused by Mr. Chambers; you realize that, doctor?"

A. "You have told me that."

Q. "Yes. Now, doctor, assuming that with the exception of going to Mr. Berle in 1939 with Mr. Isaac Don Levine, in all other cases people came to Mr. Chambers; in other words, Mr. Murphy came to him at his farm on two occasions; that he testified before the House Committee pursuant to a subpoena from that Committee; that he testified in the grand jury pursuant to a subpoena from that body; that he testified here pursuant to a command, and the FBI went to see him on other occasions—would you say that under all of those circumstances, assuming those are the facts, that they would be the action of a person accusing somebody, or would a person who was accusing go to the other people and accuse?"

A. "I think I have cited only two examples of accusation, false accusation. I know of no others."

Q. "I am asking you as a doctor, if you assumed the facts to be that the man did not go and make accusations to A, B, C, D, E and F, but people came to him and he answered questions pursuant to their command or demand, would you say that that is the attitude of a person who makes accusations as such?"

A. "I would like to be as accurate as I can. It is certainly not the attitude of a man who makes indiscriminate accusations."

Q. "Well, assuming, doctor, that over a period of many years Mr. Chambers did not say anything about espionage; assuming that he told nobody about the perfidy of Mr. Hiss until 1948 in the grand jury or in the Baltimore deposition, but that he previously, since 1939, when he was asked said that X and Y and Z were members of a Communist apparatus, and denied that there was evidence of espionage, would you say that that would be the actions of a person making false accusations?"

A. "I would not know."

Mr. Murphy: "Shall we recess now, your Honor?"

The Court: "Very well."

(Short Recess)

Mr. Murphy: "Doctor, some of the observations that you made of Mr. Chambers when you observed him at the last trial and once on this was that he had a rather vague memory for dates. Is that a symptom of anything at all, doctor?"

A. "Everything is a symptom of something, but that—"

Q. "Isn't it a symptom of being normal?"

A. "It could be, yes."

Q. "Doctor, you also pointed out that he recalled on one trip that he took with Mr. Hiss to Erwinna, Pennsylvania, over the Easter weekend there, one of the things he remembered was a policeman who had a lily in his hand on that Saturday, and you thought that was—"

Mr. Cross: "It was Easter Sunday."

Mr. Murphy: "Easter Sunday I am told."

Q. "—you thought that was a characteristic of something, but I forgot what you said it was."

A. "I said that not to remember your wedding day was extraordinary but that to remember details of that sort was also extraordinary; that it showed a strange kind of memory."

Q. "A strange kind of memory?"

A. "Yes."

Q. "Doctor, do you say that a man who does not remember the exact date he got married exhibits some sort of a symptom of psychopathic personality?"

A. "No one thing is a symptom of psychopathic personality."

Q. "Would you say that a person who remembered the month and the year after 19 years was doing fairly well?"

A. "Pretty good."

Q. "Doctor, isn't it a fact that most normal people remember incidents of the past by some strange or outstanding thing? I mean, couldn't a woman remember something by the color of another woman's hat 20 years ago which had no real relation to the fact itself except that she remembers this big feather sticking up, that sticks out very clearly in her mind—doesn't that sometimes happen with all of us, doctor, that some little thing sticks in one's mind?"

A. "Some little things sometimes help to recall others, that is right."

Q. "And a little thing by itself may have been just a very, very small part of the whole incident?"

A. "That could be true."

Q. "Now, doctor, another observation that you made was that during the time that Mr. Chambers was on the stand in the last trial and once here he appeared to have no remorse, I think you said; no remorse when he testified about the various times when he did not tell the whole truth. Do you attach—"

A. "That is not exactly what I said. When he testified to the fact that he had lied I said he showed no contrition or remorse or any apparent emotion. He did it in a sort of debonair way—'Yes, I was.'"

Q. "I think you said 'bland'."

A. "Bland."

Q. "You realize of course, doctor, or assume, doctor, that Mr. Chambers told his story to 12 ladies and gentlemen at the last trial for a period of seven or eight days; that he had previously told the story to the grand jury over many days—"

A. "You mean told that he had lied?"

Q. "Assuming, doctor, that he told the facts; bear in mind that he had been to the grand jury in October 1948 when he denied that he had any knowledge of espionage."

A. "Yes?"

Q. "And that same body of men and women heard him during the five or six or eight days, whatever the time was, in December of 1948 when he told them what the facts of espionage were; and assuming further, doctor, that he previously told it all to the FBI before he went to the grand jury, and assuming that he told it at the last trial—do you still feel, doctor, that a person who has told it so many times under so many different circumstances should exhibit outward emotions on the witness stand?"

A. "I would assume—"

Q. "I think I can ask for a yes or no answer on that, doctor."

A. "I think he should."

Q. "He should?"

A. "Yes."

Q. "Now, doctor, can you tell when a witness is experiencing the emotion, let us say, remorse sitting 25 feet away?"

A. "I cannot."

Q. "You cannot?"

A. "No."

Q. "So you don't know whether or not Mr. Chambers was inwardly feeling remorse when he told the story here?"

A. "I can only testify to what I saw."

Q. "And you cannot tell from 25 feet away what the inward feelings were?"

A. "No, I could say something about his outward manner."

Q. "Yes, but you cannot tell about remorse which is a feeling within us?"

A. "That is right, I can't see remorse."

Q. "You can't see it?"

A. "Not unless there is some outward manifestation of it."

Q. "And sometimes people have remorse without manifesting it outwardly?"

A. "That can be true."

Q. "As a matter of fact, we sometimes see it playing poker, don't we, when we say 'poker face'?"

A. "That is right."

Q. "Now, doctor, you also told the jury that Mr. Chambers had a characteristic of psychopathic personality in that he panhandled or that he showed symptoms of panhandling. Now, doctor, before I go into that do you want to withdraw that?"

A. "I didn't say what you just said. I said that panhandling was one of the symptoms of psychopathic personality."

Q. "And you said that Mr. Chambers exhibits some of those symptoms?"

A. "I said I specifically talked about his borrowing money and not paying it back."

Q. "Now, doctor, I am going to ask you whether you want to withdraw that now before I question you on it?"

A. "I would be glad to have you question me on it."

Q. "All right, let us first find out, one, is the term 'panhandling' a medical or just an ordinary dictionary term we all know?"

A. "It is a lay term."

Q. "Lay term?"

A. "Used in the literature on this subject."

Q. "And it means accosting strangers on the street?"

A. "I should think that was right, yes."

Q. "And we people here in New York are familiar with it because we are so near to the Bowery and other places where we see so many, is that correct?"

A. "That is right."

Q. "And you tell this Court and jury with all the seriousness that you can command as an experienced doctor that Mr. Chambers is guilty of panhandling?"

A. "I tell that he on two occasions to my knowledge, at least to my knowledge from the hypothetical question, borrowed money from friends and made no attempt to pay it back. I call that panhandling. If you want me to withdraw the name and call it something else, I will."

Q. "Doctor, you said you didn't want to withdraw it, and I am going to ask you whether, as you sit there before these ladies and gentlemen of the jury, as a respected member of your profession, you tell them that on the facts that were assumed in the hypothetical question in your opinion Mr. Chambers exhibits symptoms of panhandling?"

A. "Not in the sense that you are using the word, no."

Q. "Now, doctor, we have agreed on the meaning of the word. You said it was an ordinary law word, and I will read to you what you said on page 3685:

Q. Are there facts which would fall under panhandling?

A. Panhandling is one of the symptoms that I mentioned. One has the testimony of Wadleigh, that he borrowed $20 from him and made no effort to pay it back, or borrowed $10—I think Mr. Wadleigh said $20—made no effort to pay it back; and in the hypothetical question I have been asked to assume that on several occasions he borrowed small sums from Mr. Hiss, and again made no effort to repay them.

Q. Now, doctor, do you say now that when a person borrows $20 from a man that he has been friendly with for a period of a few years, like Mr. Chambers was with Mr. Wadleigh, and did not pay it back, that that to a trained psychiatrist is evidence of panhandling? Really, doctor, do you mean that?"

A. "No. I think you win on that."

Q. "Now, you stated, doctor, that Mr. Chambers exhibited a symptom of a psychopathic personality known as vagabondage, and that was because you assumed in your state of facts that Mr. Chambers after he got out of high school and was about 17 or 18 years of age, ran away from home and lived in the City of Washington and worked there, and subsequently went to New Orleans where, according to his own testimony, he lived in some sort of a dive, and subsequently returned home on money that was supplied I think by his parents through his grandfather. Now, doctor, are there other evidences in the hypothetical question which lead you to believe that Mr. Chambers exhibited the symptoms of vagabondage other than those that I have described?"

A. "That is the only one."

Q. "Doctor, a boy who runs away from home in the year 1920, whatever the year was then, and who returns in a period of three months, who works, supports himself for a while—is that really evidence of vagabondage?"

A. "One piece of evidence, yes."

Q. "That is the only evidence that you have?"

A. "That is right."

Q. "Doctor, haven't there been rather famous people who have run away from home and who have made quite a success of themselves?"

A. "I am sure there have."

Q. "Dick Wittington became Lord Mayor of London, didn't he?"

A. "I think so.

Q. "Benjamin Franklin ran away from home."

A. "Did he?"

. . .

Q. "How about Al Jolson? He ran away from home. Would you say that was evidence of a psychopathic personality?"

A. "I don't know anything about Al Jolson's personal life."

Q. "Well, doctor, you said another symptom was the fact that he was untidy. Seriously, doctor, a person who is untidy, does that mean that they are manifesting a symptom of psychopathic personality? Can you name dozens of people who are untidy who are respected members of our community?"

A. "I can't name dozens whose—"

Q. "Well, let's see."

A. "—whose mouth was described as filthy, who testified—?"

Q. "Well, we will come to the teeth in a second. Would you describe Professor Einstein as a well dressed man?"

A. "I have only seen him once, and on that occasion—"

Q. "He had a sweatshirt on then?"

A. "No, that was the tercentenary celebration at Harvard, and he was dressed up for the occasion."

Q. "He was dressed up for the occasion?"

A. "That is right."

Q. "How about Will Rogers? Do you know Will Rogers?"

A. "Oh, sure."

Q. "A fastidious fellow, was he?"

A. "I never looked at his linen. It wasn't described as filthy, as it was in this case, or dirty."

Q. "Heywood Broun? Do you remember Heywood Broun?"

A. "A classmate of mine."

Q. "Tidy or untidy?"

A. "Oh, dirty."

Q. "Bing Crosby?"

A. "I don't get around as much as you do, Mr. Murphy."

Q. "Doctor, that is not evidence of a psychopathic personality, is it, how a person dresses?"

A. "No."

Q. "No?"

A. "Never said it was."

Q. "Now, doctor, lastly, you said that one of the things that you attach importance to was the fact that Mr. Chambers had unstable attachments. That is one of the real characteristics, isn't it, of psychopathic personality?"

A. "It can be."

Q. "Doctor, in all seriousness, as a man who has been out of medical school since 1914, do you tell us that Mr. Chambers has no stable attachments when we know, and you have assumed, that he has been married to the same woman for 19 years?"

A. "I did not say he had no stable attachments."

Q. "Well, if he had stable attachments—and that is a stable attachment, isn't it?"

A. "It can be."

Q. "Well, it is, doctor, isn't it? 19 years? Won't you concede that being married to the same lady and being the father of her two children and living with her for 19 years is cogent evidence of a real stable attachment? Won't you concede that, doctor?"

A. "I have known marriages that have lasted longer than that that appeared to be stable and weren't. I don't know the nature of their marriage. I am perfectly willing to assume what you want me to assume."

Q. "Yes. Assume that, doctor, and then tell us, as a professionally trained man, whether that is evidence of a stable attachment?"

A. "If you ask me to assume that it is a good marriage and that he has stuck to this one woman as you describe, of course that is evidence of a stable attachment."

Q. "As a matter of fact, a marriage of 19 years is one of the best evidences of stable attachments, isn't it?"

A. "Of that kind of attachment, yes."

Q. "Doctor, assume that Mr. Chambers went with *Time* magazine in 1939 as a book reviewer and over a period of almost ten years rose in that organization until he became one of the six senior editors, at a salary of $30,000 a year, and during that time worked hard for that magazine, wouldn't that also be very cogent evidence of a real honest-to-goodness stable attachment?"

A. "In that particular instance, yes."

Q. "Now, doctor tell us, please, in seriousness, what you considered in the hypothetical question Mr. Chambers' unstable attachments were?"

A. "To the Communist Party, to the United States—"

Q. "Well, let's see. He was not attached to the Communist Party with any degree of stability, is that what you mean?"

A. "He was in and out of it."

Q. "Let us see. Assume, doctor, that he joined it as a junior in college, in 1924 or 1925, and he left the Communist Party in 1938; assume further that he was the editor of the *Daily Worker*; assume that he was editor of the *New Masses*; assume that he worked almost for nothing, that sometimes he got $10 a week and sometimes nothing; assume that he was paid $25 a week and $35 a week when he was a paid functionary of the Party; assume that he went underground for them and during all of that time had no other positions; assume, doctor, that from 1924 or 1925 until 1938 that was his only job, wouldn't you say, whether his philosophy was right or wrong, that it was a rather firm attachment to that cause?"

A. "I was referring to the fact that he was in the Party, out of the Party, in the Party and out of the Party."

Q. "Well, doctor, you are referring to some dispute in 1925, when the Lovestonites got out and the Stalinists came in; is that what you are referring to?"

A. "When he got out, yes."

Q. "Well, he didn't get out. He said he sulked; he went and never gave up his card. He was, and I think you said yourself, that part of the testimony was that he felt he was as good a Communist as Stalin?"

A. "Better."

Q. "Better. So it is not in and out?"

A. "I understood that it was."

Q. "Well, assuming that it was not, doctor, that he was a Communist to the core commencing from the day that he told Professor Van Doren, down to April 1938."

A. "Well, I wouldn't call that an unstable attachment."

Q. "Now, what else did you say was an unstable attachment, based upon the facts in the hypothetical question?"

A. "Oh, I talked about his career at the public library, his career at Columbia, his episode at Williams. With respect to these institutions he was there and gone, and sometimes back again."

Q. "Well, let us see, doctor. When a boy registered at Williams, assume that he went there for two or three days, decided that it was not the place for him either socially or economically, and left almost within a matter of three days. You don't describe that then as an attachment, whether unstable or stable, do you?"

A. "You are right."

Q. "And in Columbia, he left and came back by virtue of the fact that he had written this offensive play?"

A. "Came back by virtue of that fact?"

Q. "Sorry, sir?"

A. "You say he came back by virtue of that fact?"

Q. "No. He left, as I understand it, in his sophomore year—"

A. "Yes."

Q. "— by virtue of that fact. And he came back, he was not expelled; he just left of his own and he came back and stayed for part of his junior year. I think that is the testimony. Do you say, doctor, that a man who attends only part of three years at college exhibits unstable attachments? There must be thousands of those people, aren't there?"

A. "I don't know how many."

Q. "Well, don't you think, doctor, from your experience as a New Yorker, that you feel that there must be literally thousands of people who don't finish college?"

A. "Oh, certainly."

Q. "And you don't say that they have unstable attachments when they leave college in the middle of their college career, do you?"

A. "They could have. I wouldn't know."

Q. "But there are so many different reasons why people leave college?"

A. "That is right."

Q. "Now, what other factors did you say—oh, the library. How long was he working with the library before he was fired, under your assumed state of facts?"

A. "A fair number of years. I can't remember the exact number."

Q. "Well, until he was fired, that showed an attachment to the library?"

A. "Until he was fired, yes."

. . .

Q. And that is the evidence from which you say Mr. Chambers had unstable attachments, and one of the symptoms which caused you to say he had a psychopathic personality?"

A. "That is right."

Q. "Now, doctor, did you say that there was some evidence of psychopathic personality when a person has bad teeth?"

A. "No."

Q. "So we can't attach any medical importance to that as far as psychiatry is concerned?"

A. "Yes, we can."

Q. "What conclusion do you draw from a person who has bad teeth, psychiatrically speaking?"

A. "If the bad teeth are the result of neglect—"

Q. "They usually are, aren't they?"

A. "Usually."

Q. "Yes."

A. "And if the neglect is the result of not going to a dentist and have proper hygiene done. I would certainly attach some significance to that."

Q. "Not too much?"

A. "Some. Certainly a man who earns $30,000 a year shouldn't have what is described as a filthy mouth unless he has some particular feeling about going to the dentist to have his teeth—"

Q. "It was in 1943, wasn't it? And he had his teeth fixed in 1942? And it was recently that he made $30,000? He was just coming up?"

A. "You mean he didn't have enough money to go to the dentist?"

Q. "No. I am trying to find out what medical significance it was, and you said that you think a man who makes $30,000 and doesn't have his teeth fixed exhibits some evidence."

A. "That is right."

Q. "If you assume, doctor, that it was in 1943 that Mr. Chambers was described as having a filthy mouth and it was at that time that he had dentures and extractions, would you say that that was some evidence of psychopathic personality?"

A. "Yes, I think that degree of neglect of one's self is some evidence."

Q. "Is some evidence?"

A. "That is right."

Q. "So that all people who neglect their teeth would be exhibiting some evidence of psychopathic personality?"

A. "No. That is like your question about running for the midnight train. It has no meaning. You have to take everything into consideration."

Q. "Well, doctor, taking everything into consideration that you have told us about on cross-examination, do you tell us now, as a trained psychiatrist, that in your opinion Mr. Chambers is suffering from a disorder of character known as psychopathic personality?"

A. "Most certainly."

There is little to quibble with concerning this cross-examination except the last question. An expert rarely changes his opinion and does not here. I would not ask the last question and argue the opinion is without basis in closing argument. This is the approach noted in the earlier chapter on cross-examination, Section 9.1, Attacking Opinion, which suggests getting only what you need for your closing argument.

The jury rejected Dr. Binder's opinion.[1] Hiss was convicted and sentenced to five years in prison. Whitaker Chambers wrote a famous autobiography called *Witness* and was a part of the rise of the conservative wing of the Republican Party. Richard Nixon, who had chaired the subcommittee to determine whether Hiss or Chambers were lying, became the vice president for Eisenhower shortly after this affair. Thomas Murphy became a long-serving Federal District Judge and died at the age of 89.

In 1995, the year that Thomas Murphy died, the Central Intelligence Agency and National Security Agency made public the "Verona Papers," which seemed to implicate Hiss as a Soviet agent. Hiss maintained his innocence throughout his life and had many supporters.

---

1. One may wonder how Dr. Binder was permitted to testify by the District Court Judge Goddard since Dr. Binder was arguably invading the province of the jury by, in effect, opining on a witness's credibility. The answer is in footnote 12 of *U.S. v. Ianniello*, 740 F. Supp. 171 (1990), which, 40 years later, observed:

> It was the oft-expressed philosophy of Judge Henry W. Goddard of this Court (who served from 1923 to 1955) that a defendant in a criminal trial could adduce any "evidence" he or she wishes to present to the trial jury. This was thought to provide greater fairness and minimize reversals. Judge Goddard carried his rule to the ultimate extent when he permitted the witness Dr. Binder to sit in the second trial, which lasted from November 17, 1949 to January 21, 1950 and observe the mannerisms and conduct of Whitaker Chambers in the courtroom, and then opine to the jury that Chambers was a pathological liar.

For those interested in Judge Goddard's reasoning, see 88 F. Supp. 559 (S.D.N.Y. 1950). It is doubtful Judge Goddard's Rule would be followed in courts today.

About the Author

Alan Radnor is a retired partner in the Vorys Columbus office. As a trial lawyer, he specialized in the presentation and advocacy of medicolegal issues. He represented both defendants and plaintiffs in medical malpractice, toxic torts, and personal injury cases throughout Ohio in both state and federal courts. Mr. Radnor also represented hospitals and medical staffs, drafted medical staff bylaws, worked with physicians on medical staff selection issues, and advised physicians on medical ethics. Mr. Radnor is a Fellow of the American College of Trial Lawyers.

Career highlights include:

- Successfully prosecuted the first Ohio case determining birth certificate paternity in an in vitro fertilization case
- Successfully defended asbestos manufacturers in jury trials involving asbestos-related diseases, including mesothelioma
- Successfully defended one of the first litigated fear-of-cancer cases
- Received record plaintiff's verdicts in four Ohio counties

Mr. Radnor has spoken extensively on a variety of topics, including medical malpractice, legal and ethical issues in medical genetics and pediatrics, brain death protocol, communications in the courtroom, and the linguistic aspects of jury instructions and professionalism.

Mr. Radnor received his J.D. cum laude from The Ohio State University Michael E. Moritz College of Law, where he was a member of the *Ohio State Law Journal* and the Order of the Coif. He received his MS from The Ohio State University, and his BA from Kenyon College.

INDEX